"The advancement of AI and web developn. erated pace. Author Todd Korpi helps us to be proactive and think critically and ethically on how AI can help the church remain missionally effective."

Doug Clay, general superintendent of the Assemblies of God

"As Christians, we must engage with technology wisely, trusting that God is sovereign over all advancements, including AI. In *AI Goes to Church*, Todd Korpi offers a thoughtful perspective on integrating AI into ministry while upholding theological and ethical integrity. At Jesus.net, we see AI as a tool to enhance evangelism and discipleship, not replace human connection. This book challenges the church to approach AI with faith, wisdom, and responsibility. I highly recommend it to leaders seeking to navigate AI's role in spreading the gospel."

Jan-Willem Bosman, CEO of Jesus.net

"In this unprecedented era, when technology is transforming every aspect of life, the church can't afford to lag behind with a dial-up connection to a high-speed world. Our God certainly isn't standing still. In *AI Goes to Church*, Todd Korpi offers a bold and necessary vision for how Christian leaders can embrace AI, not as a threat but as a powerful tool for ministry, discipleship, and social impact."

Kyle Lee, director of strategy for Indigitous US

"Todd Korpi's book highlights a critical reality: churches and ministries need to proactively engage AI, balancing opportunities with concerns. Measuring impact and using data to inform church programs is essential, and AI is becoming a vital tool for gathering and analyzing data to improve decision-making. Years ago in a talk, I shared, 'The world is changing fast! And today is the slowest rate of change we will ever see,' emphasizing the urgency for ministries to adapt to the needs around them; AI can make this easier, and Korpi helps leaders get comfortable with AI."

Kate Williams-Whitley, president and chief impact officer of EIG Insights

"As artificial intelligence infiltrates more areas of life, questions arise about how to approach these creations while remaining focused on God. *AI Goes to Church* explores AI not from a consumer perspective but a compassionate one. Todd Korpi encourages us to consider how these tools can glorify God and help others. This enthralling, timely book is full of biblical wisdom and compassionate insight. Anyone interested in the intersection of technology and faith should read *AI Goes to Church*."

Dave Ferguson, CEO of Exponential and author of *B.L.E.S.S.* and *Hero Maker*

"Here is an informed, wise, and pastoral resource, knowledgeable about the opportunities and challenges of AI, discerning about its potentialities and pitfalls, and attentive to the divine invitation to flourishing extended to frail human creatures. Todd Korpi is a sure guide for those seeking to understand and engage AI in the mid-2020s."

Amos Yong, professor of theology and mission at Fuller Theological Seminary

"Given the scale and pace at which AI technologies are advancing, it's impossible to know precisely what our techno-future holds. In *AI Goes to Church*, Todd Korpi wisely resists the urge to predict the future and instead focuses our attention on what people of faith can do in the present to leverage AI technologies for the sake of God's mission in the world. It's a faithful and generative approach that will be helpful for Christians of all stripes, regardless of how much or how little they know about the possibilities and pitfalls of AI. I highly recommend it."

Kutter Callaway, author of *Techno-Sapiens in a Networked Era* and associate dean at the Center for Advanced Theological Studies at Fuller Theological Seminary

"AI isn't coming—it's already here, reshaping the way we live, work, and even minister. *AI Goes to Church* is the guide we need to navigate this new reality with both wisdom and conviction. Todd Korpi doesn't just explore AI's potential; he thoughtfully wrestles with its ethical and theological implications, never losing sight of the Great Commission. He bridges the gap between abstract philosophy and real-world ministry, helping the church engage AI with both faithfulness and practicality."

Charlotte Sanchez, chief communications officer of the Luis Palau Association

"*AI Goes to Church* is the book the church didn't know it desperately needed. With clarity, humility, and pastoral wisdom, Todd Korpi offers a compelling framework for engaging artificial intelligence with theological depth and missional courage. This is not just a book about technology—it's about discipleship, mission, and the future of the faithful presence of the body of Christ in a digitally hybrid world. I'm grateful for Todd's voice and wisdom. I highly recommend this book to pastors, educators, and anyone wondering what it means to be effective ministers in a digital age."

Mark Pettus, lead pastor of Church of the Highlands

"Clearly, AI will change the world. And it will also change us. As people of faith, we have an essential role to play in using and shaping AI in alignment with our values. In *AI Goes to Church*, Todd Korpi brings thoughtful insight to the questions we all should ask while he helps us toward the answers."

Scott Beck, CEO and cofounder of Gloo

TODD KORPI

AI
GOES TO
CHURCH

—— PASTORAL WISDOM ——
FOR ARTIFICIAL INTELLIGENCE

FOREWORD BY ED STETZER

An imprint of InterVarsity Press
Downers Grove, Illinois

InterVarsity Press
P.O. Box 1400 | Downers Grove, IL 60515-1426
ivpress.com | email@ivpress.com

InterVarsity Press® is the publishing division of InterVarsity Christian Fellowship/USA®. For more information, visit intervarsity.org.

All Scripture quotations, unless otherwise indicated, are taken from The Holy Bible, New International Version®, NIV®. Copyright © 1973, 1978, 1984, 2011 by Biblica, Inc.™ Used by permission of Zondervan. All rights reserved worldwide. www.zondervan.com. The "NIV" and "New International Version" are trademarks registered in the United States Patent and Trademark Office by Biblica, Inc.™

While any stories in this book are true, some names and identifying information may have been changed to protect the privacy of individuals.

Published in association with the literary agency of WordServe Literary Group, Ltd., www.wordserveliterary.com.

The publisher cannot verify the accuracy or functionality of website URLs used in this book beyond the date of publication.

Cover design: Faceout Studio, Jeff Miller
Interior design: Jeanna Wiggins
Images: © Massimo Merlini / E+ via Getty Images, © Andriy Onufriyenko / Moment via Getty Images

ISBN 978-1-5140-1124-9 (print) | ISBN 978-1-5140-1125-6 (digital)

Printed in the United States of America ♾

Library of Congress Cataloging-in-Publication Data
Names: Korpi, Todd, 1986- author
Title: AI goes to church : pastoral wisdom for artificial intelligence /
    Todd Korpi.
Description: Downers Grove, IL : IVP, [2025] | Includes bibliographical
    references.
Identifiers: LCCN 2025006636 (print) | LCCN 2025006637 (ebook) | ISBN
    9781514011249 paperback | ISBN 9781514011256 ebook
Subjects: LCSH: Artificial intelligence–Religious aspects–Christianity |
    Artificial intelligence–Moral and ethical aspects
Classification: LCC BR115.T42 K67 2025 (print) | LCC BR115.T42 (ebook) |
    DDC 253.0285/63–dc23/eng/20250428
LC record available at https://lccn.loc.gov/2025006636
LC ebook record available at https://lccn.loc.gov/2025006637

32 31 30 29 28 27 26 25 | 13 12 11 10 9 8 7 6 5 4 3 2 1

To the laborers in the fields:

pastors, missionaries,

church planters, faithful saints.

May you never grow weary

in doing good.

CONTENTS

FOREWORD

ED STETZER

TECHNOLOGY IS EVOLVING at an unprecedented pace in our age, and the church stands at a crossroads. Artificial intelligence (AI) has transitioned from the realm of science fiction to an integral part of our daily lives. AI influences how we communicate, make decisions, and even perceive the world around us. In light of the rapid advancements of AI, faith communities are presented with the question of how they should respond and engage.

On the one hand, Christians proclaim a timeless and unchanging gospel. The mission Jesus has given to the church has not changed for two thousand years, no matter how society changes. As I often say, "The moment we're in does not change the mission we're on." On the other hand, the New Testament also models wisdom in responding to the changes of the moment. We don't change just to change. But in wisdom, we communicate the gospel more effectively so that all the world may know Jesus as Lord. All Christians before us experienced this tension between the timelessness of the message and the timeliness of the moment, and we must also steward this tension faithfully in our own cultural contexts.

AI technologies are evolving rapidly, and thus Christians will wrestle with significant issues just as rapidly. We want to respond to these issues well, so we must engage them thoughtfully and biblically—while remaining committed to sharing and showing the life-changing gospel of Jesus Christ to a world that desperately needs him.

In *AI Goes to Church*, Todd Korpi explores how to faithfully navigate this very tension. He has put in the work to gain a deep

understanding of how theological principles relate to technological advancements, bridging the gap between ancient faith
traditions and modern innovations. Todd balances optimism and
caution. He doesn't call us to blindly celebrate AI as a tool to
optimize ministry efficiency or to reject it wholesale.

Instead, Todd challenges us to consider the deeper theological
and ethical implications of using AI. For example, how do we
maintain the integrity of pastoral care when chatbots can mimic
human empathy? How do we ensure that AI-driven applications
gift us back our time so that we can steward it for the sake of the
gospel and meaningful connection with others? Such questions
aren't easy to answer, but we must face them to live faithfully in
the moment.

AI Goes to Church is not a book of ways to optimize your use of
AI applications. Neither is it a book of theological or missiological
ideations without real-world impact. I've known and worked with
Todd for years, and I appreciate his heart to bridge deep thoughtful
reflection with practical ministry impact. This book builds such
a bridge. It will benefit Christians who want to be faithful in the
complexities of the moment *and* provide an enduring collection
of perspectives on how the church can harness the power of
digital technologies to make disciples of all nations.

Most strikingly, this book at its core is not about technology—
it's about people. Todd reminds us that AI, like any other tool, is
only as effective as the hands that wield it. He warns us against
approaching AI with uncritical fear or enthusiasm, instead calling
us to discernment, wisdom, and a commitment to the mission of
God. This book is a call to see technology not as an end but as a
means to glorify God and serve our neighbors.

AI Goes to Church will benefit anyone seeking to navigate the
digital frontier with faithfulness and integrity. We stand on the
cusp of unprecedented technological change. This book challenges us to consider how we can leverage AI for kingdom

purposes, ensuring that our commitment to the gospel remains unwavering as technology advances. I'm confident that *AI Goes to Church* will inspire you to engage with the digital age thoughtfully, embracing the opportunities it presents while steadfastly upholding the timeless truths of our faith.

1

A BRAVE NEW WORLD

AS A CHILD COMING OF AGE in the late '80s and '90s, I was enthralled by *Star Trek: The Next Generation* (TNG). Gene Roddenberry's hit sequel ran for seven seasons between 1987 and 1994 and told the tale of the legendary flagship USS *Enterprise*, captained by stoic and heroic Frenchman Jean-Luc Picard. Being a part of the generational subgrouping frequently dubbed "elder millennials," TNG hit the airwaves at the height of my childhood imaginary years. I was smitten.

In addition to the battles with Klingons and Romulans, the technological offerings of the twenty-fourth-century starship fascinated me: a laptop computer, sitting on the desk of Picard's ready room, that seemed so slender by the standards of the day; the "Personal Access Display Devices," or PADDs (that at some level were undoubtedly an inspiration for our modern iPads and tablets), the ability to travel faster than the speed of light, and more.[1] And, of course, there was Lieutenant Commander Data.

On the *Enterprise*, Commander Data was a mainstay. The embodiment of the android before Google was even a thought, Data was a physical embodiment of an artificial intelligence (AI). Even by twenty-fourth-century standards, he was a technological marvel—sentient, capable of vast computation that rivaled the *Enterprise*'s onboard computer system, and capable of evolving and growing in a semblance of personhood. While an AI, Data was also on a lifelong quest to grow into being more human, and many plotlines within the franchise leaned on the ethical considerations of such a quest (e.g., Can an android command a starship?). Subsequent movies and spinoff series introduced new practical and ethical considerations, such as the introduction of Data's "emotion chip" in the motion picture *Star Trek: Generations* in 1994.

You may or may not have been as Trek crazy as I was in my early childhood, but chances are shows like *Star Trek* and *Black Mirror*, and movies like *Star Wars*, *Avengers: Age of Ultron* (2015), and others shaped many of your expectations about what a future with artificial life forms might look like.

But it is increasingly apparent that much of what Gene Roddenberry and George Lucas anticipated for the distant future (or a long time ago, in a galaxy far, far away) is breaking into the present. The technological developments made within the digital age have had such a compounding effect that what would have been considered massive technological breakthroughs thirty years ago are often nothing more than little blips in the news cycle:

"Oh cool, they may have discovered a path toward an unlimited fuel source—that's nice."[2]

"Hey hon, did you see that my AirPods have a 'Live Listen' feature that can turn your phone into a hypersensitive directional microphone?[3] Anyway, what do you want to do for dinner?"

I was ten years old when the Roslin Institute cloned the first mammal, a Finn-Dorset sheep named Dolly. It felt like that was all anyone could talk about when they weren't talking about the 1996 Centennial Olympic Games. Yet when I read about advances in the field of in vitro gametogenesis (IVG)—a technological advancement that has the possibility to turn any human cell into egg cells capable of fertilization (and consequently, life)—in an issue of the *New Yorker* in 2023, no one I talked to seemed the least bit impressed, or even interested.[4]

Technological advancement is so commonplace that it produces a sort of white noise effect. Until we stumble onto its usefulness, it feels like a steep—and potentially futile—learning curve to which one must commit. After all, not all technologies are here to stay—such as the early 2010s partnership between Nokia and Microsoft that was supposed to revolutionize the smartphone industry. Most North American homes have at least one box somewhere with outdated cords, old phones, and maybe even a VCR, should one get the inspiration to watch some old home movies.

If we're not careful, we can also find ourselves grossly behind on some technological advancements that are likely here to stay and that may wield tremendous influence on both our individual lives and on human civilization as a whole. It is difficult to closely follow every tech advancement so, for many, the debut of ChatGPT in November 2022 by developer OpenAI probably seemed like a massive leap that came out of nowhere. If you're not familiar with ChatGPT, it is what is called a large language model AI or an LLM. That's simply a fancy way of saying that it is a bot that sources its bank of knowledge from the internet as well as the ongoing use of end users (i.e., you and me).

In the fall of 2022, I was just a pastor and a missiologist who was still struggling to get Siri to respond to my voice commands correctly, and out jumped this AI resource onto the main stage of public conversation.[5] ChatGPT made previous iterations of virtual assistants and AI seem ancient by comparison. For most of us, ChatGPT has already dramatically altered how many of us operate day to day. I readily use Chat (as well as an emerging suite of other AI tools such as Claude, Motion, Apple Intelligence, and more) for complex idea synthesizing and brainstorming—things that would have previously taken me hours, now completed in a manner of seconds.

Since the debut of ChatGPT, just about every online resource claims to be recently upgraded with AI capabilities, though many used AI before and are simply trying to capitalize on the

marketing frenzy. The possibilities seem endless and are expanding at a rapid pace. AI has the potential to be "a shift in
human experience more significant than any that has occurred
for nearly six centuries—since the advent of the movable-type
printing press."[6]

AI AND THE PEOPLE OF GOD

The relationship between technology and the Christian church
has always been evolving. While the church often gets a bad
reputation for being a late adopter of emerging technologies,
that's not entirely true—*especially* when it is used to reach
people with the gospel. It may be more accurate to say that local
churches may lag behind adopting new technologies, while the
"sodality" parts of our faith—missions agencies, evangelistic
organizations, church planting networks, and more—are at the
cutting edge of technological adoption, dreaming up ways to use
every possible means and method to reach people with the
gospel of Jesus Christ.[7]

While we often associate the word *technology* with the electronic developments of the twentieth and twenty-first centuries,
the term derives from the Greek word *technē*, meaning "art,"
"craft," or "skill." So while, yes, your smartphone is a form of
technology, so were the letters composed by Paul and sent to his
churches. When viewed in this light, Paul's letter writing was a
primitive form of "multisite" ministry, allowing him to be
simultaneously present in one location (where he was ministering
physically at the time) and present in another, with a proxy (such
as Phoebe) reading his letter to another of his churches.[8]

The Roman roadway system is another example of what was,
by the standards of the time, a monumental technological
achievement, which Christians used to spread the gospel (e.g.,
Acts 8:26-40). Later technological developments, such as
Gutenberg's movable-type printing press, the advent of radio

technology, the use of automobiles and air travel for missionary work, and the widespread embrace of television broadcasting are only a few cursory examples of where the church has been an early adopter of technological development.

The digital age has seen similar pioneering efforts as churches adopt new digital technologies early. Life.Church, based out of Edmond, Oklahoma, and America's largest church, gave us not only the YouVersion Bible app in 2008, but they also launched a virtual reality campus in the Metaverse almost as quickly as the platform became available.[9] By 2021, the YouVersion Bible app had reached more than five hundred million downloads worldwide. To date, it is an entry road into cultural contexts written off as "post-Christian" by many, such as France, where YouVersion has more downloads per capita than any other place on earth. But long before that, Christians were finding ways to connect, worship, and share the gospel online—including the first virtual worship service held on Ecunet on January 28, 1986, in response to the *Challenger* accident.[10]

Of course, for every early adopter of digital tech in Christian spaces, there are also a host of late adopters—even resisters. Among the most notable examples with regard to technology and Christian traditions are communities such as the Amish, who take a long-form skeptical approach to technological adoption. But by late adopters, I'm not so much referring to our Amish sisters and brothers as I am to the pastor who is still treating their church's social media like an online bulletin board from the '90s, existing to communicate one-way information.

I'm referring to the fact that digital technology is viewed by many church leaders as a luxury for large churches with bigger budgets and more people power. What's more, ministry that takes place *within* digital environments is largely relegated to second-class status—a peripheral ministry that often consists of posting church news on a church's official social media feed and, since the coronavirus pandemic, some form of live streaming the Sunday service. While some church leaders are jumping into pioneering feats, others are more skeptical, even developing an adversarial posture to a technology that shapes even the lives of those who don't directly participate in it.[11]

But the internet isn't a fad that's going to blow over. And by all appearances, AI and other Web 3.0 developments (e.g., virtual reality, augmented reality, blockchain, etc.) are going to further integrate the human existence into a hybrid one—constantly simultaneously online and offline—and dramatically change our lives. The winds of AI integration are blowing across human civilization, whether we want them to or not. We can choose to be reactive or proactive. As the people of God—especially those of us who are in some form of Christian leadership, whether in the local church, the academy, or in some form of church-proximate ministry—it is crucial we choose the latter path, one of conscious engagement and participation in the public conversation around how to think well about and steward this human creation.

There is already a sense of urgency to this task, as the widespread adoption of AI tools is dramatically outpacing our careful reflection and discourse on the subject. This is especially true as it pertains to the arenas of theology, Christian ethics, ecclesiology, and missiology. While in our pluralist societies, it is foolhardy and ignorant to assume that Christianity is the *only* moral voice giving guidance to these questions, it is certainly true that in both the West and the Majority World, Christianity has been a significant moral voice historically and still is at present. The question for the Christian is, then, why wouldn't we want to be a part of this discussion? In fact, why wouldn't we want to *lead* it?

If the people in our churches and in our ministries are going to use AI in greater and greater capacities as the technology evolves (and they will), isn't dialoguing about what it means to steward AI from a Christian perspective a matter of urgent discipleship? If our commission is to join the Holy Spirit in his reconciliatory mission in the world, beckoning people to be reconciled to the Father through the victory and present reign of Christ (and it is), shouldn't we explore how AI can aid in our participation in that mission?

These, and more, form the basis for why I've embarked upon composing this book. It behooves us as Christians to think theologically and ethically about what it means to live as humans in the age of AI and about the potential opportunities and challenges that may arise from its widespread adoption, both in the short-term and long-term future. Contrary to popular belief, technology is not acultural, neutral in its orientation, or immune from pitfalls that can harm vulnerable populations. We therefore must think ethically about technology from a Christian perspective.

We also must think ecclesiologically and missiologically about the proliferation of AI. We must not simply theoretically consider the ramifications of this technology, but also the very real and practical uses to aid in our work of cultivating vibrant and flourishing church communities that are on mission with God in the world.

THE PURPOSE AND CONTENTS OF THIS BOOK

Around the same time ChatGPT made its debut in 2022, I was asked to lead the research for a new collaborative effort called the Digital Mission Consortia.[12] This was formed through a partnership between ministries and institutions who are leading the way in the field of digital ministry, including OneHope, the Wheaton College Billy Graham Center, YouVersion, Talbot School of Theology, Alpha, and many more. Through that research (and the subsequent work resulting from it), equipping Christians, local churches, and ministries to engage effectively with digital technology and in digital environments has become a significant part of my life's work. AI already impacts a significant part of our lives, and its rapid proliferation only serves to forecast greater impact in the future. So the necessity for this book was clear: that it might equip you and me to better navigate living our faith in our common AI future.

In this book I address both theoretical and practical concerns around AI. In between those two spaces—idea and practice—is where I feel this work is most needed. We simply can't move forward with pragmatic recommendations for using AI, as much as the modern appetite longs for some variation of "five tips to maximize x, y, and z." We need the groundwork of *thinking* well about what we *do*. But academics are often, rightly, criticized for living too much in the realm of ideas. This book is written as a connective tissue that links idea with practice.

We will touch on the basics of what AI is and the current state of play; and then we will dive more into specific topics, such as issues around social justice, pastoral care, and what it means to be human in an age where machines can increasingly mimic human behavior and reason. We will explore some of the issues I envision as being on the horizon. Not all are topics of conversation now, but I write much of this in the hope of beginning conversations that will inevitably happen soon, so we might get a firm theological footing before we are forced to navigate them.

But since there are concerns regarding the coming impact of AI, as we will see, its impact has already been far reaching for many years, often in ways so subtle as to escape our notice. This impact is not simply in the marketplace, government, or our private lives, but AI has also come to church. It has been sitting in our seats on Sundays without us realizing it. It shapes our ministry practice in ways we often overlook. And it stands to do much more in the short-term future.

Almost weekly, I have conversations with visitors to our church who visited us because they found us online, either because our church populates high in Google (because of an AI-powered practice called *search engine optimization,* or "SEO") or because their social media algorithm inserted one of our content pieces in their feed. Simple tools we take for granted—like predictive text in Microsoft Outlook, automated audio and visual enhancements when we upload sermons in platforms like YouTube, smart scheduling tools, targeted ads, and more—AI already permeates how we function in church life as well as in the Christian life more broadly.

We need an awareness both of the present opportunities and challenges AI presents when it goes to church as well as of the future ones. What function can AI hold in good sermon preparation? How can AI create margin in your schedule so you can make a greater difference in people's lives? How can AI help you reach people you wouldn't otherwise be able to reach with the gospel? What cautions do we need to consider—such as the potential threats AI operation poses to our mandate to steward creation wisely? How do we respond to "AI friends" or bots that blur lines between personal and digital interactions? By engaging these questions, we start to see AI not just as a tool to optimize our lives, but as a call to deeper discernment and reflection about how to apply pastoral wisdom to our hybrid, incarnational-and-artificial world.

My hope in setting out on this journey with you is, first, to provide you with best practices for *thinking well* about AI and our place and calling as the people of God, and second, to know how to put that good thinking into practice. In that, I desire to make this work more "evergreen" than books on technological development often are. While I will, of course, mention examples of best practices in what I call "ministry AI," I try to steer clear of the nitty-gritty details of particular AI resources, developers, or technological practices.

I do this for two reasons. The first is that I'm a missiologist, not an AI developer. Thus, my expertise is better employed in the arena of how the church engages with the technology for the sake of the gospel, rather than the particularities of how a technology is used. If you're wanting thirty ways to maximize your use of ChatGPT, I'm not your guy and this isn't the right book. But if you're wanting to develop a foundation for how to think about AI and apply that thinking to your life, to your church, or to your vocation, then I commend this book to you in the hope that it will be beneficial.

The second reason is that technology is evolving at a rapid pace. To place much stock in a particular tech practice is to consign this work to an outdated status almost immediately. I sincerely desire to give you something of more enduring benefit, rather than something quickly lumped in with a stack of books on how to create engaging Vine videos and leverage your MySpace account to talk to people about Jesus.

Additionally, I approach this subject matter with as much neutrality and objectivity as possible. Surely, that is impossible to do completely. However, I would count myself as neither an overly eager adopter of technology nor a hard resister to it. Despite coming of age with some exposure to tech (our family got our first internet desktop computer with a dial-up internet connection when I was eleven), I am also at an age where I somewhat begrudgingly eye roll every time a new social media platform comes out, because I just simply don't want to learn a new one! Unlike my children, I have vivid memories of running to get a snack when my favorite show went on a commercial break—because there was no such thing as pausing television. Yet my high school friendships, and typing skills, were profoundly shaped by long chats on AOL Instant Messenger.

We Millennials often get a lot of undeserved bad press, but one thing our generation uniquely affords the contemporary conversations around digital landscape is a deep appreciation of the value of tech as well as its potentially disastrous consequences, having lived part of our lives before, and part after, the digital revolution.

Thus, my hope is to be as neutral a mediator as possible in this conversation. To those who may be overeager about AI's potential, my hope is that you'll see some potential cautions and guardrails to consider, lest we afflict the world with unintended consequences in our haste. To those who are reluctant, my hope is that your heart and passion for the gospel and for people will inspire you to take the ministry potential of AI more seriously and consider how you might navigate this emerging ecosystem with clarity and authority.

Not long ago I spoke at a conference for church leaders on the subject of digital ministry. This particular session was on using social media for ministry, and I was fortunate to find myself in a room primarily full of church planters, pastors of revitalizing churches, and leaders of small churches. Almost everyone in the room represented small congregations with limited staffing and limited budgets, but big vision and unquenchable passion to serve their communities.

As the conversation unfolded, it naturally turned to the ministry implications of AI, though that was not my intention for the session. We discussed how algorithms impact how people view a church's social media content. We talked about how tools such as OpusClip and Sermon Shots can turn sermon content into reels or how SpeakAI can translate that same content into a host of other languages or how Canva's AI integration can make slide deck creation a snap—all doable with a skeleton crew and a shoestring budget. The reality is that for many in that room, and for many other churches who do not have large staffs and massive budgets, the ever-expanding library of AI tools can equip churches to do ministry in cost-effective and time-saving ways. For larger churches this can mean more focused staffing on pastoral functions over execution-oriented functions. I looked around that room to see something I don't often see when the topic of digital ministry comes up—*hope*. Not a hope because of anything inherently holy about AI. But rather a hope that the AI-optimized resources can lower the threshold for churches of all sizes and varieties to participate in ministry in digital environments. That excites me.

There remain looming questions that must be addressed about our common humanity, identity, pace, work, and more that remain largely ignored, however. These are the existential questions that I have deep concerns about Christians overlooking and the church being ill equipped to respond to. These too must be addressed—thinking well *and* putting that thinking into practice, for the glory of God and the ongoing work of the gospel.

My hope is that we will walk away from this journey together with a deep conviction that God still desires to reconcile the world to himself through his Son Jesus the Messiah and by the abiding ministry of the Holy Spirit who, before we even encounter people, is already ministering to them, inviting us to discern where he is at work and to join him. I'm convinced one of the most significant frontiers in which the Spirit is at work is precisely where most of us spend a great deal of our time—in digital environments and interacting with digital tools. To that end, the Spirit of God is calling us to join him in his work in and through digital technology.

The next frontier of gospel ministry lies in digital environments and using digital tools like AI. But this requires us to think well about the relationship between AI and the people of God, so that we might promote human flourishing and dignity, and use every means at our disposal to compel people far from Jesus to be reconciled to him.

Let's see what's out there.

JEAN-LUC PICARD

2

UNDERSTANDING ARTIFICIAL INTELLIGENCE

POPULAR-LEVEL CONVERSATIONS around the implications of artificial intelligence (AI) vary widely between enormous optimism and deep skepticism—even fear. For our purposes, we need to temper both extremes to be able to more objectively examine what AI even is, and only then establish a foundation to think well about it.

First let's look at the nature of *intelligence* itself.

To some extent, the term *artificial intelligence* is a bit misleading in that to many it implies a level of internal sophistication that current iterations of AI simply do not have. For centuries philosophers have debated about the nature of intelligence— what is it, who possesses it, how do we recognize it, etc. Growing up, I thought they gave advanced degrees to people for their intelligence. However, now having earned a doctoral degree and still routinely struggling to spell *rhythm* correctly on the first try, I can tell you this is not always the case. There are different types of intelligences, and the definition of *intelligence* itself is a concept open for debate.

Mid-twentieth-century mathematician Alan Turing gave the world a way of looking at intelligence as something that should be measured "not [by] the mechanism, but [by] the manifestation of intelligence."[1] In other words, Turing asserted that intelligence can only be measured by the external behavior of a thing, arguing that "if a machine operated so proficiently that observers could not distinguish its behavior from a human's, the machine should be labeled as intelligent."[2]

This approach, later named the "Turing Test," has become a gold standard by which we measure the intelligence of machines— in terms relative to the performance of their human overlords (you and me) to perform a similar task. Today's current iterations of AI are dubbed "intelligence" not because they themselves possess intelligence in the way that you or I might have spoken about the smart kid in school, but because they are made to mimic forms of human intelligence.[3] In this way, we might say that as it pertains to AI, there is a difference between mimicking intelligence and possessing intelligence. AI is in the business of mimicking intelligence more than it itself is intelligent in an ontological sense. But for those of us not immersed in the world of technological development, we consider AI "intelligent" nevertheless because of its capacity to perform tasks in a manner similar to human beings. In no small way does AI fool us in causing us to believe it is intelligent in a way that we are intelligent, yet it is only a mimic of intelligence rather than something that possesses intelligence in a proper sense.

There are several ways technology experts classify and group types of AI. The categories used by industrial research giant IBM, however, are among the simplest to understand for those who aren't immersed deeply into the world of AI. For our purposes, we will use these categories throughout the book.[4]

Category one: Narrow AI. Simply put, narrow AI (sometimes also called "weak AI") is the sort of technology we have today. Narrow AI is programmed to execute a defined task; it leverages the curation of information to perform within defined parameters given to it. Narrow AI can perform tasks better and faster than humans. While OpenAI's debut of ChatGPT caused many to assume that AI is new, this sort of AI has been around for decades, though it has improved by leaps and bounds the last several years. Even chatbots and relationship bots, which are designed to mimic human speech and conversation, are simply a form of narrow AI. This broad category encompasses other terms like "generative AI," "large language models," and more.

Within the scope of narrow AI, IBM outlines two subtypes of technology, based on functionality. First, there is "reactive machine AI," which uses currently available data to predict or recommend future decisions. Have you ever been in a conversation where you mention something that you'd like to purchase, only to find the next time you're scrolling Instagram your ads are magically tailored to that purchase? That, and other recommendations by "the algorithm" (whether it be suggested friends on Facebook or the "shows you might like" section on Hulu), are reactive machine AI. Reactive machine AI has been a regular part of our daily lives for years now, often directing our purchases, social media engagement, and streaming preferences. It shapes our worldview more than we would ever like to admit.

The second subcategory of narrow AI is "limited-memory AI." The advances in limited-memory AI have sparked public interest so widely since the debut of ChatGPT by OpenAI. Unlike reactive machine models, limited-memory models can retain past information to inform their current and future tasks.

ChatGPT and the virtual assistants on our smartphones are examples of limited-memory AI. The rapid evolution of AI technologies in this space is awakening public imagination over the potential AI has both to massively disrupt the norms of our lives as well as to add expediency to them.

In my own work, AI has played a significant role in streamlining my efficiency. I use an AI-powered productivity planning tool to schedule and rearrange the work I complete on a daily basis. This allows me, someone who is woefully ill-suited to break down large tasks into smaller, time-bound action items, to maintain a high level of productivity while still maintaining a quality harmony between my work and the rest of my life.

Following OpenAI's release of their custom GPT feature in 2023, I created a custom GPT, a limited-memory AI version of "myself." The KorpiGPT bot has learned from my previous writing and other publicly available content and can make recommendations about future projects with ease. While I don't use the bot for the actual writing process, KorpiGPT has been an invaluable tool to help me create outlines, edit content, and be a brainstorming aid that has saved me from countless hours of staring at "the drawing board."

On the back end of a lot of my larger writing projects, I use Grammarly's masterful AI-powered resources to make recommendations in the editing process. I tend to be verbose, so Grammarly helps me trim down my word choice. I also tend to be needlessly snooty in my word choice, and Grammarly helps me temper that tendency in favor of a better blend of readability and sophistication.

So, while a bit oversimplified, these things can reasonably be said:

1. Narrow AI is *today's* AI. Everything else is theoretical.
2. Of narrow AI's subcategories, reactive machine AI has been giving order to our lives for a while.
3. Limited-memory AI, from personal assistants to self-driving cars, is what is revolutionizing our lives today.

Category two: General AI. "Artificial general intelligence" (AGI, or sometimes called "strong AI") is theoretically the next step in the evolution of artificial intelligence. AGI is a theoretical concept in which AI technology could possess the intellectual capabilities of a human, including its need to grow into its own intelligence, much like a child grows intellectually over time. Fictional depictions of AGI, both by Paramount, include Cortana on *Halo* and Zora on *Star Trek: Discovery*—two AI that are sentient and grow in their capacity to not only expand knowledge but expand in the application of that knowledge.

Unlike narrow AI, which can only perform tasks within its defined parameters, AGI would have the ability to perform new tasks outside of its original context, without human intervention. So, hypothetically speaking, an AGI tool designed as an expert in eighteenth-century French art could decide to also develop an expertise in international poverty development or could learn to compose music.

One type of AGI in its experimental phases is in what's called "emotion AI." If actualized, emotion AI would be able to detect, analyze, mimic, and respond to displays of human emotion. Think about getting home from work after a long, hard day, and Alexa recognizing your facial features, gait, and the tone in your voice and responding by proactively offering empathy, turning on what it knows to be your favorite mood-booster playlist, and perhaps even offering to DoorDash you dinner so you can kick your feet up and relax. Of course, with every possible upside, there are cautious dystopian scenarios, such as what is showcased in the episode "Help" of the 2019 Netflix series *Creeped Out*, which describes an AGI who takes license with two unruly children while their parents are away, trapping them in the house until they get along in order to teach them a lesson their distracted parents are unable to teach.[5] But I much prefer the scenario where Alexa knows that I'm sad and orders me Taco Bell to cheer me up.

Category three: Super AI. "Super AI" is a theoretical future event wherein artificial intelligence not only has intelligence capabilities that match humans, but actually *exceeds* human capability. In this future, inaugurated by what many refer to as a technological "singularity," super AI will have the ability to take up new tasks, create new things, self-diagnose and improve, and essentially exist without the need of human intervention. Here, many futurists hypothesize that machines will be self-aware, though some attribute sentience as a characteristic of AGI.

This postsingularity future seems far off, but many speculate it is much closer than we might think. The unbelievable progression of AI technology has caused some futurists to hypothesize that somewhere around 2040 to 2050, we will reach this singularity event. Whether a singularity event is fifteen years away or one hundred fifty years, it should cause Christians to take the conversation about the implications of AI seriously, and we should consider how to think theologically about what it means to be human and participate in God's reconciliatory work in the world within such a time of profound change.

TECHNOLOGICAL TERMS IN THE AI CONVERSATION

If you're like me and many others not immersed in the world of tech, the sheer volume of "inside baseball" terminology when talking about technology can be daunting. When I hear my beloved tech-geek friends nerd out about "neural networks" and "API" my eyes struggle to avoid glazing over, as I'm sure theirs do when I throw around ministry-world words like *hermeneutics* and *contextualization*.

But the technological terms used for AI are important to not only comprehend what is meant in AI conversations, but in also establishing a baseline understanding to evaluate it theologically and missiologically. To that end, I want to offer some basic definitions for words commonly used in conversations about and around AI that may be helpful to understand. If you look up definitions to these words on most tech websites, they usually define them by using equally confusing inside baseball terms (such as talking about "nodes" in defining "neural networks"). So, for our purposes, I've asked ChatGPT to provide some working definitions.

With only a little tweaking, this is what ChatGPT had to say about, well, itself:

- *Artificial intelligence (AI):* This is like giving a computer a brain. It allows computers to do tasks that usually require human intelligence, such as understanding what people say, recognizing objects in pictures, making decisions, and learning from past experiences.

- *Machine learning:* Imagine teaching a dog new tricks by rewarding it with treats. Machine learning is similar but for computers. You give the computer data (like showing pictures of cats and dogs) and let it learn over time to tell the difference, without having to explicitly program it to recognize every single cat or dog.

- *Neural networks:* Think of a team where everyone has a specific job, and they pass the ball along to score a goal. Neural networks are like this team inside the computer, made up of units (players) that pass information between each other and make decisions, working together to solve problems.

- *Deep learning:* This is like taking a deep dive into a subject. Deep learning uses very complex neural networks to analyze big amounts of data. It's like reading a book so thoroughly that you can understand themes and ideas that aren't directly stated.

- *Natural language processing (NLP):* Imagine having a friend from another country who speaks a different language, and you use a translation app to understand each other. NLP is the technology that helps computers understand and respond to human language, making it possible for us to talk to devices and for them to understand us.

- *Algorithm:* This is a recipe for solving a problem. Just like following a recipe to bake a cake, an algorithm gives the computer a step-by-step process to follow to complete a specific task or solve a problem.

- *Data mining:* This is like being a detective looking for clues in a mountain of data. Data mining involves searching through large amounts of information to find patterns, trends, and connections that aren't obvious at first glance.

- *Robotics:* If you've ever seen a robot vacuum cleaner or a manufacturing robot in a factory, that's robotics. Robotics is about building machines that can move and do tasks, often tasks that are too dangerous, dull, or difficult for humans.

- *Augmented reality (AR):* Imagine looking through your phone camera and seeing digital images appear on top of the real world, like a game character standing on your coffee table. AR combines real and virtual worlds, enhancing what you see with computer-generated information.

- *Spatial computing:* Spatial computing is like giving computers a sense of space, allowing them to understand and interact with the 3D world around us. It combines virtual reality, augmented reality, and artificial intelligence to blend digital objects with real environments, making digital interactions feel like part of our physical space.

That's not a bad set of working definitions, if you ask me. But full disclosure: I initially gave ChatGPT a prompt that directed it to target the definitions to help Christians understand these terms and it produced a list of the cheesiest Bible comparisons ever suggested (e.g., "AI is like the wisdom Solomon asked for, but for machines!").

THE HISTORY OF ARTIFICIAL INTELLIGENCE

The history of artificial intelligence parallels the history of the modern computer itself. In their book *The Age of AI*, Kissinger, Schmidt, and Huttenlocher note,

In 1943, when researchers created the first modern computer—electronic, digital, and programmable—their achievement gave new urgency to the intriguing questions: Can machines think? Are they intelligent? Could they become intelligent?[6]

However, twenty-two years earlier, on January 2, 1921, Czech playwright Karel Čapek debuted his stage production of *R.U.R.* (for *Rossumovi Univerzální Roboti* or "Rossum's Universal Robots"). Čapek painted a picture of a world in which creatures with artificially manufactured flesh and blood worked as forced labor for their human creators. These *roboti* eventually rebel and bring about the annihilation of humanity. Čapek's play gifted the English-speaking world with the term *robot*, which comes from the Czech word for "forced labor" or "slave."[7]

Before the engineers, mathematicians, and scientists create a technological marvel, the seeds of such a marvel are often sown into the soils of human cultures by poets, playwrights, and dreamers. Long before your average Gen Z was rolling around your neighborhood on a hoverboard, Robert Zemeckis and Bob Gale depicted them in the storyline of *Back to the Future Part II* (1989). We see here a similar pattern take shape in the mind and work of Čapek, who conceived of humanoid robots two decades before the modern computer was invented and over a hundred years before the merging of cybernetics with human bodies (as with Cleveland Clinic's invention of the bionic arm, complete with sensation communication to the human brain, or Elon Musk's implantation of a Neuralink chip into a human brain).

I cite Čapek's 1921 *R.U.R.* as the *cultural* genesis of AI, along with other works of the period such as Thea von Harbou's *Maschinenmensch* (German for "Machine-Human") in the 1925 sci-fi novel *Metropolis*, and L. Frank Baum's Tin Man character in his 1900 novel *The Wonderful Wizard of Oz* (which, of course was made forever popular in the 1939 film adaptation).

But many cite Alan Turing's 1950 publication of the paper "Computing Machinery and Intelligence," wherein he gave the world the Turing Test, as the formal beginnings of AI—taking it from the land of fantasy toward a conceptual framework that would allow us to scientifically measure the "intelligence" of a machine. However, Turing himself lacked the ability to provide proof of concept (computers, of course, weren't as easy—and not nearly as cheap—to come by in those days), and it wouldn't be until 1956 when Allen Newell, Cliff Shaw, and Herbert Simon introduced "Logic Theorist" to the Dartmouth Summer Research Project on Artificial Intelligence (DSRPAI) conference, that the world would have an identifiable, real-world AI program.[8]

Following DSRPAI, AI entered a period of rapid development, to the extent that computer scientist Marvin Minsky was quoted in 1970 as saying that within three to eight years the world would have an AI with the same intelligence as an average human being (a cautionary tale to those who might put too much stock in current predictions of singularity timelines).

Progress slowed in the '80s and '90s, a time referred to as "AI winter" where funding dried up and attempts at advancements were met with generally disappointing results.[9] However, this lull in AI progress was short-lived, as breakthroughs in machine learning (the capability of a machine to learn through experience) accelerated much of the current landscape of AI we take for granted in our lives today. Amid the machine learning revolution came one of the most important cultural moments in the history of AI—in 1997, when IBM's machine learning program Deep Blue beat chess champion Gary Kasparov.

Since then, through the advent of object recognition technology in the first decade of the twenty-first century, significantly greater developments have been made (while still often using chess play as proof) such as Google DeepMind's AlphaGo, which beat Ke Jie, world champion in Go (a board game more complex than chess), in 2017.[10] Whereas Deep Blue and other now-classic chess programs were developed by human play encoded into their programming, DeepMind's machine learning allows its programming to play millions of games against itself—not only developing patterns based on its own usage but also evaluating the potential moves most probable to yield favorable outcomes.[11]

AI AND THE CURSE OF THE HUMAN REBELLION

I want to return to Čapek's *Rossumovi Univerzální Roboti* and reflect theologically for a moment. I was initially exposed to the origins of the term "robot" as meaning slave through the 2017 Boyer Lecture by cultural anthropologist Genevieve Bell. While listening to her lecture, I was struck by her cursory mention of this fact. I had to pause the lectures and reflect on that thought for a bit.

While I'm uncertain as to the nature of Čapek's personal religious faith, it is clear that his vision of the human desire to manufacture an artificial labor class was prophetic in nature, both in how the world of robotics has since unfolded and in tapping into a deep human longing to transcend beyond the present toil of this life. I witnessed the fruit of this desire in the confines of my Instagram feed after Tesla featured its latest version of the Optimus robot at the "We, Robot" event in October 2024. Social media subsequently did what it is so expertly skilled at doing and produced a cascade of reels making jokes about their future personal Optimus reacting to being required to perform menial tasks or observe its human overlord's laziness.

I'm certain there will come a day, especially as strides are quickly being made in the evolution of humanoid robots, where questions emerge as to whether it is ethical at all to force humanoid robots to exist as slave labor. As AI technology advances to increasingly *look* more humanly, *seem* more humanly, and *think* more humanly, questions of whether humanoid robots

possess rights and personhood—and other ethical dilemmas—
are certainly on the horizon.

But the ramifications of Čapek's robotic vision aren't just about
future ethical conundrums. His imaginings also speak to us presently about what it has always meant for human beings to try to
transcend the reality of our need to toil in working the earth. That
begins not with a vision of a futuristic android workforce but with
the Garden of Eden.

Genesis 3 is the narrative commonly referred to as "the fall."
However, it is more appropriate to refer to it as "the rebellion." It
is the first of *three* rebellions that we find in the book of Genesis
(the other two being the fallen "sons of God" in Genesis 6 and the
Tower of Babel in Genesis 11).

The reason I believe the term *rebellion* is more appropriate to
describe what is happening in Genesis is because precisely that—
rebellion—is taking place. *Rebellion* better conveys the willful
choice involved in the unfolding of the events described, and it
also serves to remind us of its ramifications today.

The initial rebellion of humankind can sometimes be diluted
down to its basic parts, rendering it preposterous—as though the
sin of humanity was stealing fruit from the tree like a teenager
raiding the family pantry for Oreos against his parents' instruc-
tions. That's just not what Genesis has in view.

Instead, there are two opposing sources of wisdom, symbolized
in the tree of life (i.e., God's wisdom) and the tree of the knowledge
of good and evil (i.e., human wisdom). Human rebellion came as
a result of listening to the *nakhash* and electing a self-sourced
form of wisdom to carry out their created purpose in contrast to
wisdom sourced from YHWH (as represented in the tree of life).
The *nakhash*, generally translated in English as "serpent," is an
otherworldly figure (as opposed to a literal snake). It is likely not
the satan, as popular culture would have us believe, but a repre-
sentation of multiple symbols wrapped up in one including chaos,

disorder, a messenger of divine oracles, and a being with the appearance of divinity itself.[12] By this summation, the *nakhash* is essentially posing as an emissary of YHWH with a message meant to lead them toward rejecting YHWH's wisdom and following their own, which results in the chaos and disorder with which our world is afflicted today.

The resulting consequences of this rebellion are pronounced in Genesis 3:14-19, dealing with several themes:

- disorder and death (Gen 3:15)
- pain and patriarchy (Gen 3:16)
- the futile toiling for survival (Gen 3:17-19)

These consequences, resulting from the fall (rebellion) are just that: consequences. They are outside of the bounds of what God intended for creation but are, instead, a result of our choice to follow the path of our own wisdom and to reject the wisdom that is sourced from God alone. We know that the beauty of the gospel message is a heralding of the end of these very common human experiences, brought about through the victory of Jesus the Christ at the cross and at the empty tomb. John's Revelation paints a picture of a return to humankind drawing from the life-giving nutrients of the tree of life and an explicit statement that, "There will no longer be any curse" (Rev 22:3 CSB). This means

- *shalom* (wholeness or order) will be brought to the nations (Rev 22:2) and death will be forever defeated (1 Cor 15:26; Rev 21:4);
- pain will be eradicated (Rev 21:4) and patriarchy will come to an end (Gal 3:27-29; Rev 22:3);[13] and
- our toiling for survival will give way to eternal life (Rev 21:4; Rom 6:23; 1 Cor 15:35-54).

The trouble is that we find ourselves between two advents. You and I live after the first coming (i.e., advent) of Christ, where this curse was broken, and before his second coming, where the consequences of this curse will finally be defeated. As it pertains to our conversation on AI, this is important for two reasons.

Resisting the curse. First, there is something significant woven within the very fabric of what it means to be human that recognizes the consequences of the rebellion as unnatural—not in the sense that they're not a part of the human experience (which they are, universally), but that they're *not supposed to be*. Whenever we weep over the death of a loved one, something primal within our gut reminds us death is not the way things are supposed to be. Every time we feel like we can't get ahead financially, regardless of how hard we work, there is a felt sense of injustice we feel toward that hardship—it's not the way things are supposed to be.

As a result, human beings instinctively—through our perpetual innovation—create measures to mitigate the impact of the curse. We attempt to bring order to chaos in any number of areas, whether it be through the grid patterns of our city planning or in our neatly manicured lawns. Long before modern medicine, humans took it upon themselves to find ways to dull pain, such as the mitigating tactics employed to reduce the pain of childbirth. Everything from laws that criminalize the abuse of women, to the women's suffrage movements of a century ago, to measures taken to address inequalities in pay gaps between men and women recognize a need for greater equality between women and men. We inherently see efforts to prolong human life as good and do whatever we can to prolong our own and the lives of those we love.

Likewise, for thousands of years, human beings have attempted to make work easier—less toilsome, less burdensome—to widen the margin between our standard of living circumstances and the bare minimum we need to survive. From the invention of the wheel to the printing press, the cotton gin to the industrial assembly line, and more, we instinctively desire to mitigate the effects of the curse through the innovation of technology.

So Čapek's vision of the future as a time in which human beings can kick their feet up, sip some Arnold Palmers, and watch what we've created toil *for* us should not come as a surprise. In *R.U.R.*'s gift to us in the word *robot*, we find our desire to undo the consequences of our ancestral rebellion. It taps into the very essence of what *we* feel *we* must do to right a wrong that began in the Garden of Eden.

Emphasis on *we*. There we go with that human-sourced form of wisdom again.

Reversing the curse. The second reason understanding our relationship to the curse of the Genesis 3 rebellion is important lies in what the reversal of the curse through the victory of Christ means for the people of God and our work throughout our local communities and the world.

Some will point to Christ's reversal of the curse (1 Cor 15:20-28; Rev 22:3) as a future point at the end of days, but not now, as though God's people should be content wallowing in the curse of human rebellion. But this woefully misunderstands the nature of what the victory of Christ means for us today.

The operative theological term to describe where we are in the grand scheme of Christ's great reversal is "inaugurated eschatology." *Eschatology* is the study of the final things. *Inaugurated* refers to something being introduced or beginning. In other words, in this "in between two advents" time (also called the last days), the final things have been set into motion but have not quite reached their fullness yet.

It's like when a doctor prescribes you antibiotics to treat an illness. That illness is not expelled from your system the moment the antibiotic is first taken. Instead, there is a process of treatment where the antibiotic runs its course throughout your body. When you're on antibiotics you can simultaneously notice the effects of the cure while still also feeling the effects of the illness. It isn't until the regimen has run its course that the illness is finally defeated.

This is similar to how the ramifications of Christ's resurrection are felt throughout the earth. Christians *know* death is defeated, yet we still experience death now while holding fast to the expectation that, when Christ returns, death will finally die. We "feel" the effects of our healing while also feeling the sting of our illness.

In the in-between, while we wait for the final defeat of death, Christians work with the end in mind. This (and not a random proof text like Jeremiah 1:5) is why Christians should embrace an ethic that promotes the dignity and flourishing of human life, from the womb until one's final breath. Recognizing that the resurrection put a bullseye on death's chest should compel Christians to align with efforts in the in-between to cause human life to flourish.

A crucial component to Christian engagement in the world today, and our participation in God's reconciliatory mission in creation, is this "working with the end in mind." Like a painter putting to canvas the vision she sees in her mind's eye, Christians work in partnership with the Spirit to make very real those words, "Your kingdom come, your will be done, on earth as it is in heaven" (Mt 6:10). It isn't that we bring the kingdom *for* God, nor do we labor on his behalf, as though God outsourced the work to us. Instead, we work in concert with God as he brings his kingdom, aligning ourselves with his wisdom and discerning together where he is leading us to labor alongside him. In fact, the essence of the gospel message cannot be broken down into a formula. Rather, the message we herald is that, in Christ, the curse and the principalities and powers that prop it up have been put on notice. The proclamation of the gospel is also embodied through the demonstrated action and incarnational living of God's people.

Choosing a tree. We recognize now that the evolution of AI is an expression of a deeply encoded, instinctive desire within us to mitigate the effects of the curse—namely, to lessen our toil and outsource the burden of human labor onto our own creations. In this light, and at its most basic level, AI's emergence into our lives is similar to the invention of the wheel or any other technological advancement throughout history designed to do the same. At the same time, we recognize that the reversal of the curse comes not through human ingenuity, but through the finished work of Christ at the cross and at the empty tomb. We can't innovate our way out of the curse. We can only come to Jesus. We hold that Christians are called to orient their lives, their theology, their ethics, and their communities around the coming kingdom— working now with the future end in mind.

So where does AI fit in with all of this? Is it good? Is it bad?

For Christians, the answer lies not within the technology itself, but (as with so many things) our motivation and stewardship of it in the process of engaging AI. It lies not in simply how much easier AI can make our lives, but how it impacts the vulnerable, those on the margins, the poor, the environment, and more. Like the dilemma in the Garden, the issue wasn't so much "what fruit to eat" (i.e., whether we should use AI) as it was what tree from which humanity should source its sustenance (i.e., are we using AI while depending on God's wisdom or human wisdom?).

There are a couple of unfortunately ironic realities about the fruit of human wisdom. The first is that Čapek's robot slave force envisions a posture toward artificial labor that is identical to the posture of the gods in ancient Near Eastern creation myths. The gods, whether through a cosmic dispute or slaying one by another, created the world. Then they created humankind as an afterthought to slave over the land so the gods could kick their feet up (and, of course, mess with humans when they got bored). If we're not careful, AI allows us the ability to make ourselves little gods, patterning ourselves after the cruel deities of ancient Mesopotamia.

Another ironic reality about the fruit of human wisdom is how ultimately futile our work has proven to be, time and again.

There is no amount of wealth you can build that cannot be taken from you in a flash (ask both the Romans and Romanovs). No wall you can build (digital or physical) cannot be scaled, torn down, or tunneled under. Our instinctive desire to insulate ourselves from the curse through our own empire building is ultimately futile.

Last, and most importantly, the vision of Čapek (and I would argue the vision for much of the tech revolution of the last hundred years) has been to advance technology to *lessen the load* on humans. The fruit of human wisdom promises us a future where we can work less while technology works for us.

How's that working out for us?

In what universe has technology given us *less* to do and not simply given us increased capacity to do more?

Forget for a moment about AI specifically and just think about the advent of the internet—something as simple as email. Collectively, humanity sends roughly two billion emails daily: emails containing messages that even fifty years ago would have to be delivered by internal office memos (distributed by humans), letters sent through the postal service (again, distributed by humans), or simply left unsent. A simple exchange of a couple of emails can do in a few minutes what might have taken several days of correspondence a couple generations ago.

Technology has promised us that this accelerated efficiency would give us our time back. More holidays, more time with our families, more time fishing, more time with friends, etc. But instead, we've simply filled the void with more *work*. Has the time saved by our use of email instead of memo and letter writing caused us to do less work or more work in less time? We create new technologies to lessen the burden of toil, only to return time and again to our toil. Being more efficient isn't always a bad thing, but it is worth noting that the workless utopia that each new technological advancement promises to us is a mirage.

The second tree, the tree of life, represents God's intent for humans to flourish under his wisdom. The metanarrative of Scripture shows us a tree of life at the beginning of our story (Gen 2:9) and at the end (Rev 22:2), compelling us to work in concert with God's wisdom and the direction of the Holy Spirit as we walk the path between Eden and the new Jerusalem. This path considers how we leverage AI for the sake of human flourishing, for the advancement of the gospel, and for the cultivation of God's shalom in the earth.

AI is not inherently bad, nor is it inherently good. It's not a boogeyman, promising us a dystopian future where the robots have taken over (as Čapek's play concludes), but it's also not the silver bullet that is going to bring heaven to earth, ridding us of all our toil. Instead, it is the basket we bring with us as we pick the fruit from our chosen tree. The question before us is, from which tree are we going to source our sustenance? Toward which vision of the world are we going to labor? Through whose wisdom will we operate? God's or our own?

TYING IT ALL TOGETHER

Christians should care about AI, not because we need to hop on the latest technological bandwagon—not even because AI can potentially make your ministry and your life more streamlined and efficient (though it can). We should care about AI—enough to first know what it is, how we got here, and what foundational implications we should think through—because it presents enormous, complex theological challenges for us to consider. While understanding the terms that define AI is helpful (and necessary), understanding AI drills down into deeper, more existential questions that have less to do with the coding that comprises an algorithm and more to do with understanding what AI is *to us*. How we answer that question is ultimately up to us.

3

SCRIPTURE AND THE CHALLENGE OF MODERN TECHNOLOGY

A WHILE AGO, A GOOD FRIEND of mine posted a question about fasting to a ministers' group of which I'm a part on Facebook. It was the beginning of the new year, which I've come to affectionately refer to as "evangelical Lent" since many evangelical churches observe some sort of fasting period at the onset of a new year. The question was,

> When talking about fasting, do you believe it specifically has to be pertaining to food or do things such as social media fasts count as well? Bonus points too for backing up your position with Scripture.

My friend's question was undoubtedly provoked by conversations with young adults he leads in his ministry context, and it's a valid question to ask. But what got my wheels turning was the final sentence, "[Back] up your position with Scripture."

Christians are a people of the Book. We hold Scripture in the highest esteem, though we may not always agree on the finer points of things like inerrancy and canonicity. Most Christians would agree that they desire to have ethics, doctrines, and ideologies that are shaped by the Bible.

However, I have found that forming an opinion or doctrinal stance from the Bible can easily slip into something resembling the proverbial game of telephone (i.e., when a group of people line up and relay a message one by one, and each person whispers it into the next person's ear, inevitably resulting in a breakdown of the message along the way). What starts as a well-intentioned desire to hold the Bible in high esteem can, if we're not careful, actually result in doing violence to Scripture.

Though we might be well intentioned, we can treat the Bible in a misguided way—like a Holy Wikipedia from which we need only to hunt for the chapter and verse to prove our point true. We can treat it like a Magic 8 Ball, shaking it a bit for a randomized answer to whatever problem we're going through. We might even use it to prop up our own opinions, like a folded-up piece of paper under the leg of an uneven café table. So long as we can point to a chapter and verse, we claim to be "standing on the Word of God." But the question remains, is approaching Scripture in this manner standing on the Word of God? Or is it—if we're indeed honest with ourselves for a moment—actually misusing the Word of God to our own advantage?

ANCIENT TEXT, MODERN ISSUES

Growing up I often heard fiery preachers talk about how the answers to *all* of life's questions can be found in the Bible. While I believe in the truth of that statement, we cannot find the answer to all of life's questions through cherry picking disconnected bits of Scripture and manipulating those texts to make the Bible say what we want it to say. Instead, we must see Scripture as a cohesive whole, speaking to us in its themes, movement, cultural nuances, spaces *between* the verses, and reception by the whole body of believers throughout time and space. Scripture speaks to us in more living and active, four-dimensional ways than incomplete popular proof-text practices.

Some of the difficulties with this proof-text form of Scripture interpretation are revealed when we are faced with modern questions. It feels right to find a proof text to answer questions we bring to the Bible. But how do you cite, chapter and verse, the answer to a question about social media, for example, from a text that was written twenty centuries before the printing press was invented? How can you reasonably pluck a verse or two from Paul's writings to speak to God's thoughts about artificial intelligence (AI) when those verses were written to people who couldn't imagine electricity, let alone AI?

Our modern life is filled with cultural frameworks that would've been unthinkable to the ancients who first heard the Scriptures read aloud to them. The technological dimension of our culture is certainly one of those. If you were to travel back in time to first-century Palestine and brought so much as an electric toothbrush with you, you would've been hailed as a marvel (or maybe a demon). People in the village in which you parked your DeLorean would tell tales of your visit for generations to come.

If you're an American, you have probably at one point or another witnessed the failure of proof-text hermeneutics when someone inevitably attempts to make Ecclesiastes 10:2-3 a political statement: "The heart of the wise inclines to the *right*, but the heart of the fool to the *left*. Even as fools walk along the road, they lack sense and show everyone how stupid they are" (emphasis mine). Such a use of Ecclesiastes would be laughable if it were only posted by your distant aunt on Facebook, but I've witnessed that verse be used as proof-text evidence of why Christians should vote Republican *from the pulpit* in churches and from Christian organizational leaders attempting to rally their brothers and sisters around political causes.

Certainly, we can treat the Bible like a Magic 8 Ball, giving it a good shake (or Google search) and ask it, "Where in the Bible does it say how I should vote?" I might conclude that

Ecclesiastes 10:2 is saying what I need to hear (especially if it's what I *want* to hear) and conclude by and by that Jesus wants me to be a Republican. After all, it's *right there in Scripture.* Admittedly, this Ecclesiastes example is an extreme one. But other cherry-picked verses are far more pervasive and very, very common. I believe that proof-text hermeneutics are how many Christians in America develop most of their ethical, doctrinal, and ideological frameworks. And while it may be well-meaning, it is often anything but taking the Bible seriously.

But I'm convinced that the Bible still has *a lot* to say, even about modern life. The problem is not the Bible, but rather our approach to the Bible. How we approach a piece of written literature matters. If I read a poem expecting historical and factual precision, I will wind up disappointed. If I force a recipe I find online to also answer the questions of how to distribute my financial investments, I'll likely end up making some poor decisions. Likewise, the way we approach the Bible matters a great deal in the answers we get from the Bible. We often don't get the right answers from Scripture because we're coming to it with the wrong questions. This leads some to cherry-picked verses, while others dismiss the Bible as irrelevant to what they're searching for. Both are misguided.

TIMELY AND TIMELESS TRUTH

I believe the Bible has plenty to say about modern issues, even technological ones like AI, if we only approach the Bible with the right questions. This is a part of what it means to see the Bible both as *timely* as well as *timeless*. The Bible is *timely* in that it was written to specific cultural groups in a specific time in a specific geographic setting. The worldview of the people groups of the Bible were vastly different from those of us in the West (and still quite different to those in much of the Majority World today). Many aspects of the Bible speak to people in those *timely* settings.

That doesn't mean we can take a Sharpie and cross out those verses because they're of no relevance today. Instead, we need to look at *why* and *how* the Bible is speaking to those cultures, to inform how God might speak to us in our modern situations.

For example, we might consider Paul's challenge to the women of Corinth to continue wearing their head coverings when they are speaking in the assembly (i.e., the church service). Most Western Christians see this as a culturally specific directive, but that doesn't mean it has no applicability today. Instead, when we look at the *why* and *how*—why is Paul saying this and how is he going about saying it—we can identify themes of consideration for public witness and community harmony, of restraining our own liberties at times for the conscience of those around us. When we examine the whys and hows of passages like these, alongside Paul's discourses about not eating food sacrificed to idols, we can identify themes that emerge that can inform how we live today. So while I agree with the interpretation that head coverings aren't for today, the *why* behind it—that women and men alike should prioritize the health, witness, and the harmony of the church above their own individual rights—still applies for us today.

When we understand the why and the how behind the text, we can see the themes emerge from the text that make Scripture timeless. Sometimes those themes are, indeed, plain as day. "You shall not murder" is a timeless principle—but it is not timeless solely because you can point to a chapter and verse. Instead, this specific chapter and verse gives us an explicit glimpse into a larger theme to which the entirety of Scripture makes clear: human life matters to God, so it should matter to us as well.

I was first introduced to the often-quoted proverbial phrase, "the Bible was written *for* us, not *to* us," by my late friend, Old Testament scholar Michael S. Heiser.[1] I think that snappy line has real power to it. With force, it reminds us that the Bible was written to someone else—our spiritual mothers and fathers. It has been passed down through the ages, like a family heirloom, entrusted that we will steward it with the holy awe it deserves. But unlike a family heirloom, it is indeed just as much for us as it was for them—but that doesn't mean it won't take a little work to understand its application. The popular assumption that the correct interpretation of Scripture is the one most plainly available is completely absurd, lazy Christianity. No, interpreting Scripture well takes work but it's work worth doing (see 2 Peter 3:16 for a proof-text substantiation!).

A MORE EXCELLENT WAY

If we're going to develop a biblically informed framework about modern issues, we need to ask different questions of the Bible. We need to stop asking, "Where in the Bible does it say . . ." and begin asking, "What is the Bible saying?" That probably sounds overly simplistic. But most people approach the Bible with a "where in the Bible does it say" set of questions instead of a "what is the Bible saying" set of questions.

"Where in the Bible does it say?" demands Scripture meet us on our terms.

"What is the Bible saying?" demands that we meet Scripture on its terms.

Coming to Scripture on its own terms requires reading the Bible as one cohesive narrative (often called a "metanarrative"). The Bible may be a collection of books and letters compiled over the centuries, but that does not mean it is like a collection of encyclopedias, each volume disconnected from the next. The Bible may have chapter and verse markers (added centuries after its initial composition, mind you), but that does not mean it is to be read like a set of legal stipulations in a contract to which a person can point for enforcement purposes.

Instead, the Bible is story, from first to last: God's story and our story. It is our ancestry, our lineage. Yes, even the seemingly boring genealogies are part of our story—our spiritual "AncestryDNA" if you will. The story of the Bible is primarily concerned with God's heart to reconcile people to covenantal relationship with him, and how to live in covenant together as his people under the lordship of Jesus our Messiah. If you and I silence our own agendas and sit in the stillness with Holy Scripture, we can hear its words leap off the pages and testify to the story, like Sister Sally leaping from her pew to testify in an old-school Pentecostal church.

When we read the Bible as one cohesive metanarrative, proof texts become less important. But be forewarned, when those still stuck in a proof-text hermeneutic ask, "Yeah, but *where* in the Bible does it say that?" they don't take simply handing them a whole Bible as an acceptable proof text. Trust me, I've tried!

If we're to theologize well, and theologize biblically, about the questions modern technology poses, we must learn to see the Bible with fresh, holistic eyes. This not only poses a challenge to the proof-text hermeneutic, but to rigid approaches to traditional, Western hermeneutics as well. While a historical-grammatical hermeneutic certainly has value, if overrealized, it runs the risk of systematizing the Bible into a text for analysis, from which we can yield "objective" (i.e., Western) conclusions about God. If we're not careful, this approach can strip the Bible of its wonder and bar the door of our hearts from allowing its mystery and beauty to transform us. That's an unfortunate, and unnecessary, loss to bear.

THE BIBLE AND MODERN TECHNOLOGY

Before we dive into some considerations for approaching scriptural interpretation to make sense of the questions raised by modern technological advances, I want to discuss some of the dilemmas that are either currently being raised or that I am convinced will be raised in the future, as AI becomes more sophisticated and integrated into the regular goings-on of our lives.

The dilemma of theological anthropology. The increased sophistication of AI, especially as it is embedded into anthropomorphic forms (e.g., humanoid robots, such as Tesla's Optimus, or relationship bots like Replika or Character AI), will inevitably provoke questioning the uniqueness of humankind. For Christians, this is inextricably linked to our theology of the image of God and what it means for humans to be those who bear it uniquely. I believe this is an issue of such substantial importance that I've devoted the entirety of the next chapter to it.

The dilemma of the creator's rule over creation. Also, and likely to be brought about by the anthropomorphic shape of AI in the future as well as its capacity to be self-aware and self-improving, there is a hermeneutic dilemma on the horizon that, to some extent, already exists with digital technologies in general. That is, Christians struggle at times to see digital environments as a legitimate realm under the reign of Christ.

We typically relegate digital technology to the periphery of local church ministry, failing to fully grasp its missional potential as a frontier to minister to people. We tend to view digital technology as a luxury means of ministry, fit for megachurches and large parachurch organizations with large budgets and highly specialized staff instead of a nonnegotiable means of ministry today. In our own personal use, we engage digital worlds for self-expression, influence cultivation, commerce, relationships, and entertainment—and, of course, arguing with family and friends from high school about politics. But despite the tremendous potential of digital environments to be a mission field to which we are called, only a small fraction of Christians use it this way (posting passive-aggressive Scripture verse memes on Facebook doesn't count). I'm convinced that the overwhelming reason for this lack of missionary engagement online is that most Christians simply don't think about digital environments as a place for that. We assume that people don't change their minds about anything online, so anything we talk about is just shouting into our own respective echo chambers. But that is hardly the case.

As such, we struggle to fit digital technology properly into our framework of the rule of Christ over all of creation, which must necessarily include digital creations. This already poses issues concerning AI and other digital tech. If digital creation is *not* under the rule of Christ, then Christians have no good reason to assume any morality, any ethics, any benevolence, or any goodness at all has a right to exist in digital environments. Instead, it is the distant and dark elephant graveyard about which Mufasa warns Simba in *The Lion King*. It is beyond the reach of God's goodness and, therefore, a place where any sort of depravity and evil rightly belongs. If it is not under the reign of the kingdom of God, it is the dominion of the kingdom of darkness.

However, I don't believe this is the case. Digital environments in all forms are under the reign of the kingdom of God, because *all* of the created order, including that which is created by human hands, ultimately derives from and belongs to God. AI and other digital technologies, therefore, cannot be detached from the church's broader set of ethics and considerations of how to engage the culture to which it is called.

The dilemma of sin. Defining sin is a debated topic among Christians, largely shaped by one's church and cultural tradition. As a White American male who grew up within a predominantly White Pentecostal church, I came of age thinking of sin as wholly an individual issue. The ideas of "systemic sin" and "corporate sin" were challenging concepts for me to digest in my twenties as I began to develop relationships with thoughtful Christians from other cultures and other church traditions who thought about sin both as an individual issue as well as a corporate and even systemic issue. I'm thankful for the influence of these thoughtful believers in my life, as their perspective better aligns with the perspectives of the people groups who first received Scripture—people who would find our penchant for individualism and privatization both odd and even a bit ungodly.

Even now, the function of AI poses a challenge to modern, overly individualized concepts of sin. If AI commits an atrocity, disadvantages a people group, or harms an individual, who has committed the sin? For example, in the case of an AI-piloted vehicle killing a pedestrian, we already wrestle with questions of who to blame (e.g., is the blame on the owner of the car who wasn't paying attention? The car company whose programmers made an error in the coding? The maverick entrepreneur billionaire who owns the car company and fast tracked the car to market without proper field testing?). Has anyone *sinned*? And, if so, who? One might attribute something like a roadway tragedy to nothing more than an accident, and she or he might be right. However, in the case of more pervasive issues more harmful to society, such actions cannot be dismissed as purely accidental.

Take, for example, the use of AI algorithms on social media platforms, which are already attributed to the dramatic rise in depression, self-image issues, and suicide ideation among youth. This affliction is well-documented, and the role of social media platforms in perpetrating it is well-established. In his book *The Anxious Generation*, Jonathan Haidt cites that major depression has skyrocketed 145 percent among teenage girls since 2010 and 161 percent among teenage boys.[2] Among college students in the same time period, Haidt cites a rapid increase in a host of mental health categories: anxiety (up 134%), depression (106%), ADHD (72%), bipolar disorder (57%), anorexia (100%), substance abuse (33%), and schizophrenia (67%).[3] More than one maverick billionaire has had his day before a congressional committee to discuss it. Yet Christians are largely silent on the issue, though one can hardly argue that a terrible sin isn't being committed against our children and the God who has fashioned them in his image. I don't suggest this silence is out of a lack of care, but rather out of a felt lack of wisdom for how to prophetically address the issue.

Like the ancient practices of Molech, who demanded the sacrifice of children for his satisfaction, we seem content with the sacrifice of our children on the altars of an extreme form of neoliberal capitalism—driven by AI algorithms that provoke agitation, unhealthy comparison, and conflict in our children so that a billionaire mogul's company can afford to bring us the latest and greatest virtual reality headset (as well upgrade his private spaceship, of course).

Where do we lay the charge of sin? Certainly, we can lay it at the hands of the tech mogul and the developers. But we're only fooling ourselves if we don't also possess some of the responsibility in that sin as well. But we have yet, as far as I can tell, to truly theologize around the corporate and systemic nature of technological sin—especially in how AI allows us to commit those sins from a distance, seemingly letting us off the hook for them.

OUR CREATED PURPOSE

For us to develop a framework by which we attempt to think biblically about modern questions posed by AI and other digital technologies, we must consider Scripture as one cohesive metanarrative, as I described before. The Bible is one divinely inspired story describing God's unfolding redemptive plan for his creation and how his creation is to live in covenant with him and one another. Thus, while most Christians consider the canon of Scripture itself "closed" (i.e., we have what we have and don't add to it), there is a sense in which the story is still unfolding in the lives of God's people today.

We do not stand objectively outside of the story, inspecting it like scientists in a lab. Rather, we're called to enter into and pattern our lives after the covenantal story between God and his people. This is our inheritance, handed down to us generation after generation until it has at last been handed to us—a great family heirloom entrusted to us both to steward honorably and to be a compass by which we orient our reality today.

My friend Jesse Stone, theologian-in-residence at OneHope, frames the biblical metanarrative by pointing to the origin of everything—the creation narrative, and specifically the creation mandate of Genesis 1:26-30. He identifies three characteristics that give shape to how we live out our created purpose in light of the biblical story:

1. Kingship: we're purposed to live under God's rule.

2. Kinship: we're purposed to live together as God's people.

3. Priesthood: we're purposed to steward God's presence.

Everything in the biblical story is shaped by these three characteristics. And the Christ event is the culmination of these three characteristics taking up residence in the Human One, Jesus the Messiah. He not only perfectly embodies divinity but also perfectly embodies humanity—showing us a "New Way to be Human" (to borrow from the so-named 1999 Switchfoot smash hit).

The task of the church is, therefore, to pattern ourselves after these three characteristics, modeling this call to be most human, as we were originally intended to be. We do this, of course, by remaining steadfastly anchored in Jesus, the risen Messiah, whose power keeps us from drifting aimlessly with the tides or capsizing in the storms.

When we approach the Scriptures, we keep this primary call to pattern ourselves in the Jesus way in focus. Through this lens, we read the Scriptures—embracing fully our call to

- live rightly under God's rule (which shouldn't be confused with establishing "Christian" governments and calling it "God's rule," which has been the unrighteous siren song of the church for centuries);
- live together as God's people (which shouldn't be confused with living as a collective of individuals who gather once a week but are otherwise disengaged from any shared life with one another); and
- steward God's presence (which shouldn't be confused with the routine performance of ritual nor the conjuring of emotional expressions during worship services).

TOWARD A HOLISTIC HERMENEUTIC

As we seek to interpret Scripture through this lens, we must consider what a more holistic hermeneutic looks like—one that supports and sustains this lens. To that end, I want to offer several hermeneutic principles that support a holistic interpretation of Scripture and will then offer a case study from Scripture that ideally embodies a better approach to interpreting Scripture. These principles are not meant to be isolated from one another or cherry-picked to retain those that sound nice and discard those that sound too difficult. They are, instead, to be inextricably intertwined practices that give shape to our humble approach to Scripture.

A hermeneutic of **shalom.** *Shalom,* though frequently translated as "peace," is better rendered as "wholeness." It is both a concept that compels us to frame our present choices and an eschatological lighthouse, giving us a beacon of God's design for all of creation. This type of wholeness is a sort where nothing is broken, lacking, or incomplete. Everything is as it should be under the providence of God's good wisdom.

Possessing a hermeneutic of shalom means that we grasp tightly to the eternal truth that God desires his restoration and wholeness to pervade every human life, every plant fiber and animal, our societies, our systems, and indeed the whole world—and we orient our interpretation of Scripture around that.

A Spirit-led hermeneutic. Within the testimony of the nascent church, we see a clear and abiding reliance on the Holy Spirit for illumination and direction. The direction of the Spirit helped early Christians discern what was good and right between them in a time of unprecedented change. We have the privilege of reading the book of Acts while perched atop two thousand years of Christian tradition, giving us an unconscious assurance that we can read Scripture rightly. But we neglect to see how risky the hermeneutic of the early Jesus sect of Judaism was—rereading thousands of years of Jewish hermeneutics in light of a resurrected Jesus that many were alive to see with their own eyes (1 Cor 15:6). There was no playbook—no precedence. They were utterly and completely reliant on the leading of the Spirit.

A community hermeneutic. The Spirit-led shape of hermeneutics cannot be done well in isolation. We overlook a valuable gift the Lord has given us in the discerning of truth as a church community. The function of the community in the process of understanding and interpreting Scripture *and* the role of the Holy Spirit in superintending that process cannot be divorced. The Holy Spirit's leading and the discernment of the community of faith function together. They are a permanent pair in the hermeneutics process, like pizza and ranch dressing to Midwestern Americans.

The phenomenon of private "devotions" is relatively new and, I would contend, a relatively anemic expression of Scripture engagement when it is the only form a person practices. While reading Scripture alone has value, the insights gained in private devotion should be eclipsed by the shared interpretation of the community. In the process of bringing interpretive dilemmas to the community "table"—wrestling with them, arguing over them, reconciling over them, and more—the Christian community is strengthened.

A hermeneutic of wisdom. J. De Waal Dryden notes that while knowledge informs the intellect (the cognitive dimension of a person's worldview[4]), "Wisdom seeks to shape human life . . . the whole person is [therefore] engaged in the hermeneutical process. When we enter the circle of the text looking for wisdom, we bring our whole person: beliefs, convictions, devotions, hopes, and fears."[5]

Reading the Bible for wisdom is about possessing what Augustine of Hippo called "ordered loves." Or to use Aristotle's understanding of human agency, wisdom is the development of a coherence between our actions, the reasons or justification for our actions, and the desire behind our actions.[6] Wisdom is understanding how to properly apply knowledge. Scripture seeks to cultivate this internal harmony in our lives (which the ancients referred to as virtue), so we should seek to pursue this wisdom with everything within us (see Proverbs 4).

TYING IT ALL TOGETHER

The Jerusalem Council in Acts 15 gives us a fascinating example of how the early Christians worked out a "frontier" issue, informed by the Jewish Scriptures while not beholden to a proof text. The Torah gave very little in the way of a clear roadmap for how Gentiles should live when they decide to follow the Messiah. This phenomenon was such uncharted territory that Paul, Barnabas, and others traveled from Antioch to Jerusalem to seek the wisdom of the leadership and develop a unified response.

We should take note, at the onset, of the response of the Antiochian church. They sought to solicit the wisdom of the Jerusalem body to bring shalom to their disrupted situation. They appointed Paul and Barnabas to seek out that external council. Upon their arrival, the group entered into a process of community discernment until Peter stood up and gave what has all the appearance of a Spirit-directed word from the Lord. Peter appeals to no Torah proof text, but instead leverages the wisdom of the Hebrew Scriptures, keeping chiefly in mind the shalom of not only the Christians in Antioch, but also their relationship with the broader church. He recommends a prescription that both avoids needless offense to Jewish believers while removing needless barriers for Gentiles to enter the faith. The Jerusalem church then sends a delegation to deliver their verdict, which is met with clear evidences of the Spirit at work (Acts 15:32) and a focus on the missional work ahead of them (Acts 15:35).

In the example of the Jerusalem Council, we see both an absence of pithy proof texting and the presence of tremendous, biblically formed wisdom. This serves as an example for us in the digital age. While we may not be wrestling over issues like circumcision, we do face uncharted ethical and moral dilemmas where proof texting simply will not do (nor will it honor Scripture's wisdom appropriately).

Instead, we should consider what it means to pattern ourselves after the apostles' conduct in Jerusalem, informing our current dilemmas with wisdom and ethics formed by the whole council of Scripture and with the whole council of the community of faith as led by the Spirit of God. When we take this posture, we can easily see both the potential to address the questions of our time with ancient spiritual wisdom *while* also recognizing that this is not an easy task. It is messy, filled with imperfection and even failure. (We see a breakdown in the unity of the church at the very end of Acts 15!) But in the process of wrestling through these questions together, remaining discontent with easy and overly pragmatic answers, we strengthen our bonds as Christians and leverage the collective wisdom and discernment capabilities of the whole church to tackle the dilemmas of the day.

I'm convinced that this is the only way we can properly discern how to live as the people of God in the age of AI. The specific dilemmas and considerations AI presents may be new, but the collective wisdom of the church is not simply ancient, but timeless in its agile application—making it perhaps the ideal source of wisdom for the age of AI.

4

AI AND THE IMAGE OF GOD

THE EXISTENCE OF ARTIFICIAL INTELLIGENCE (AI) naturally provokes within us reflective questions about what it means to be human, which often makes its way into our forms of artistic expression. This reflection was a feature of the plotline of the 2013 film *Her*, starring Scarlett Johansson as the operating system Samantha, with whom Theodore (played by Joaquin Phoenix) develops a friendship, and eventually falls in love. Other cybernetic characters such as Ava on *Ex Machina* (2014), Jarvis (Vision) on *Avengers: Age of Ultron* (2015), and Alice on *Subservience* (2024) depict similar blurred lines between the artificial and the human, provoking the imaginations of viewers and introducing complexities into a question that was once fairly simple: What does it mean to be human?

While television and film media are hardly the basis of establishing a theological framework for AI, these examples and more highlight the deep questions that demand theological reflection. All media are forms of communication. They provoke cultural questions, express cultural values, introduce frameworks for dialogue, and more. They possess the capacity to articulate cultural values and even solidify dominant, agreed-upon ideologies in a way that rational argumentation does not.

Popular media is one of many outworkings of how a society shapes its "mythic" dimension—that is, "any real or fictional story, recurring theme, or character type that appeals to the consciousness of a people embodying its cultural ideals or by giving expression to deep commonly held beliefs and felt emotions."[1] A myth does not necessarily need to be true to be powerful (it also does not need to be fictional to be considered a "myth," contrary to how we often use the term in everyday language). Myths express how we make sense out of the universe and model acceptable and unacceptable behavior and belief in a culture.[2] Myths both consciously and unconsciously express what we believe about faith, existence, humanity, and purpose through "action, drama, dance, painting, carving, and architecture"—and I would add, film, television, and digital media.[3]

Why does this matter? Because we can see how—as technology (and AI in particular) has grown more sophisticated—books, television, and movies have explored deeper and more imaginative themes around the subject. In more complex ways, we wrestle through what AI means for human existence, first through the stories we tell ourselves as a society, and only then through the technologies that actually make those stories a reality.

Early media depictions of AI forms include HAL 9000 in Arthur C. Clarke's 1968 classic novel *2001: A Space Odyssey* and even to some extent, the rudimentary questions of a sophisticated human creation in Mary Shelley's 1818 *Frankenstein*.[4] As artificial intelligence and robotics have become more at the forefront in the public imagination, films like *A.I. Artificial Intelligence* (2001), *I, Robot* (2004), *Ex Machina* (2014), and more have beckoned us to imagine a world in which human and machine coexist, or potentially break forth into conflict.

Coinciding with these imaginative depictions have come advances in technology that seem to reach for them, such as the emergence of virtual assistants like Amazon's Alexa and Apple's Siri in the 2010s, and AI "companions" such as Replika, ElliQ, and Character AI in the 2020s, which seek to mimic the growing relational dynamics of human-to-human relationships, even including romance.

In other words, our culture is searching for answers to what AI means for the nature of being human. And while the church does not possess the capability to be the singular voice that settles these questions, our ability to contribute to the conversation, thereby shaping how our cultural myths form around questions concerning AI and other human creations, is enormously important.

In wrestling with the human-AI question, we must start not with AI but instead with humanity. What does it mean to be human? Fortunately, the Jewish-Christian tradition addresses that question at the very beginning of our shared scriptural story.

WHAT DOES IT MEAN TO BE HUMAN?

The book of Genesis was not intended to be a science textbook. The creation story was not meant to answer the questions twentieth- and twenty-first-century readers have demanded of it. It was not intended to be a play-by-play, chronologically accurate account of the scientific process by which God created the material world. This should be no more obvious than in the fact that the sun, moon, and stars—the celestial objects by which humankind has measured our days—were not created until the fourth day.

Genesis 1–2 is just not as straightforward as those who demand a "face value reading" of the text might desire. Part of reading Scripture well means that we read Scripture in acknowledgment of the genre and context in which it was written. We read Proverbs differently than we read Acts—not because one is any less authoritative than the other but because we recognize that Wisdom literature requires a different interpretative posture than the sort of prophetic-historical account that is Luke's account of Acts.[5] Otherwise, we must take as a literal prohibition the warning against gazing headlong into a glass of red wine while it sparkles instead of understanding it as a caution on the perils of alcohol abuse (Prov 23:31).

To say then that Genesis 1–2 is not a scientific account is not a "low view" of Scripture. Quite the opposite. It is approaching Scripture humbly as a gift from God to his church to steward, rather than a dictionary of proof texts from which we can lift pet doctrines to peddle to the masses.[6]

The question remains, if the creation account is not a scientific account, what exactly is it? Citing John Walton, I answer that question in my book *Your Daughters Shall Prophesy*: "The story of creation was not meant to tell the story of the material origins of the universe. Instead, when the ancients spoke of something coming into existence, they were referring to its functional origins—that is, how it was set apart for a purpose."[7]

We do this in our culture as well. Is it inherently wrong to speak of a business "existing" when it files for incorporation with the government? No. But generally when we speak of a business existing, we are referring to when it is open for business—when it has been set on course for its purpose.[8] This does not mean the former is wrong, but the latter is legitimate as well, and likely more common. If a pastor plants a church, there is a long process of filing legal paperwork, raising a budget, and building a core community—this is the work of church planting. I have friends on every continent who sometimes spend years in this phase of church planting before ever holding a service open to the public. Yet we tend to speak of a church as having been "planted" once it begins holding Sunday services. This does not discount the work in the planting process but demonstrates how we understand something as "existing" once it is set apart for its intended purpose. This is what we see in Genesis 1–2.

At the climax of the creation story are humans, which the author of Genesis says have been set apart to steward creation on God's behalf, expanding the flourishing of the garden throughout the rest of the world under the wisdom and direction of YHWH.

YHWH makes a declarative statement that gives us a crucial insight into our own function:

> Then God said, "Let us make humanity in our image to resemble us. . . ."
>
> God created humanity in God's own image,
>> in the divine image God created them,
>>> male and female God created them. (Gen 1:26-27, CEB)

What does all of this have to do with AI? To think ethically and theologically about AI, we must understand what it means to be human. All this framing of Genesis 1–2 is important to our project for several reasons.

First, the creation narrative focuses on teleological origins—that is, the origins of the function and purpose of creation. The point of the creation story is not so much to explain the mechanics of *how* we were put here so much as it is describing *why* we were put here. At the climax of the story emerges humankind's purpose—to steward and expand sacred space as coequals, women and men together. With the heavenly hosts watching from YHWH's divine throne room, he sets humanity apart from the rest of creation as the ones designated to reflect his image.

This word for "image" is closely related to the word for "idol"—an image of something lesser that is intended to call to mind something greater. In the Old Testament, an idol of Baal or Asherah was meant to be a stand-in representative of the "real" thing. When one looked at the stone or wooden idol, one called to mind the god that idol represented on earth. What's more, the idol was often thought to be a conduit of the divine presence and power of the represented god. In the ancient Near East, such stone or wooden representations would also be erected by Mesopotamian kings in places where they wanted to establish their authority.[9]

Therefore, we see the expressed function of humankind is to function as the "idol" or image of God. It is a designation given to the whole human project, women and men equally. As Imes says, "Together we are God's image. God designed men and women to provide companionship to each other and work side by side in the world."[10]

So, the unique function of humankind is to reflect the image of God.

Second, and related to the first, it is important to underscore that the image-bearing designation assigned to humankind is an externally sourced designation. It is assigned by God to humanity. Certainly, it is true that humans have attempted, both inside and outside of the church and throughout history, to call into question the legitimacy or equality of that designation within particular people groups, but the dignity and worth of the human being as one created as God's image is something given by God alone.

Old Testament scholar Michael S. Heiser notes that image-bearing has often been associated with internalized qualities of a human such as the capacity for reason, emotion, ability to commune with God, sentience, communication, presence of a soul or spirit, conscience, free will, and indeed—*intelligence*. To use these "abilities" or "properties" to justify our image-bearing status, a host of issues results. First, nonhuman beings possess some of these qualities. (My Golden Retriever possesses a measure of intelligence. Does this mean he bears the *imago Dei*?) Second, some humans possess these qualities in greater or lesser measure. (If someone is incapable of speech or has a limited capacity for reason due to mental impairment, are they less of an image bearer?)[11]

Instead of a status or designation that arises from ability or property, the image-bearing status is one all humans inherently possess, regardless of who they are, what their perceived capacity or worth is to society, or even their salvation. Even those who do not know or reject that they are created as God's image are created as God's image and deeply beloved as his sons and daughters, though they may be estranged from his family.

So we see that (1) humanity is created for the purpose of bearing God's image and (2) image status is a designation given by God alone. Both of these points are a necessary foundation if we are to understand the AI's place as its increased sophistication challenges, as it most assuredly will, our fundamental concepts of what it means to be human.

THE IMAGE OF GOD IN THE AGE OF AI

Our task together is to establish a foundation upon which we can think on AI theologically, ethically, and missiologically. The eventual convergence of humanoid robots—such as NASA's Valkyrie, designed for humanlike operations in space and on Earth—with AI is a foregone conclusion.[12] The conceptualization of sophisticated AI embodied in a humanoid form has long been the dreams of movie and television producers, and it is only a matter of time before our technology catches up.

This necessarily requires that Christians discern carefully and prayerfully how such advances in technology challenge our traditional understandings of what it means to be uniquely human. While it seems a fanciful statement to suggest now, we will undoubtedly soon face questions related to the human-ish nature of AI. Such questions may potentially be:

- If AI reaches a point of sentience, is it more or less human? Or at the least, can it be considered a "being"?
- Should AI "beings" be granted rights under the law?
- Should a human be punished for grotesque treatment of an AI?
- Is AI-generated pornography—which contains no images of real humans—still immoral?

- Should pastors recommend AI companion bots to quell a person's loneliness? What about those bots that have "romantic partner" capabilities?
- Can my AI friend "get saved"?

The anthropomorphization of AI is perhaps currently demonstrated no more acutely than in the rise of AI companion bots, such as Replika, now widely available in your smartphone's app store.[13] The genesis of Replika came from the mind of developer Eugenia Kuyda, who thought of an idea that would eventually become Replika while she was grieving the sudden loss of her dear friend Roman Mazurenko to a hit-and-run driver while crossing the street in 2015.

In her grief, Kuyda found herself rereading her old text exchanges with Mazurenko to feel a semblance of the connectedness that was stripped from her. This led her to consider the possibility of memorializing Mazurenko within a "living" bot that would replicate his speech patterns and style. She fed both her messages with Mazurenko, as well as others provided by other friends, into a neural network to create a bot that functioned as a cybernetic mirror of Mazurenko.

This eventually led to Replika, which is designed as a blank slate of sorts, upon which users can cultivate an AI friendship that learns the user's preferences, styles, opinions, and dreams. It is designed to ask questions that provoke users to open up about themselves and their deepest feelings.[14] For those who have never used a bot like Replika, having a friendship (or romantic relationship, if one is willing to pay the price for the premium plan) with an AI sounds ludicrous. But the makers of Replika are finding that people form deep and personally meaningful bonds with the bot, opening up to it in a way that is more difficult in human-to-human interactions where fear of shame, judgment, or reprisal limit complete authenticity. While developing a relationship with a human requires taking the risk that the person may eventually betray your trust, this is not true of an AI bot—and for many, avoiding that risk is worth foregoing the human component of a relationship.

These sincere feelings of relational intimacy felt by a person toward an AI companion will most certainly introduce future questions such as those presented above, especially when an anemic theology and ethic of the *imago Dei* is driving such questions. When we consider that Gen Z and Gen Alpha are statistically both the most depressed and loneliest generations and the generations who are most engaged online, we can reasonably conclude that these ethical dilemmas and existential questions will be coming to a youth pastor near you very soon. But lest we think AI companions are a young person's game, bots like ElliQ are addressing a similar loneliness void among senior adults.[15]

We must therefore consider the rapidly emerging anthropomorphic nature of AI in light of our discourse concerning what it means to be created as the image of God. Our determination that AI (and whatever category we assign to AI in the future) cannot become truly human must draw a hard line on this matter. Out of everything in the Genesis account that was created, only humanity is set apart as being created as the image of God. We do not possess the authorization to place this designation on anything that is not human.

If we're to affirm the image-bearing status humanity possesses by virtue of God's providence and authority, then we must affirm that "humanness" is not something that can be attained, but rather an ontological (concerning one's innate being) and teleological (concerning one's function or purpose) designation given by God. Thus, to the great lament of Lt. Commander Data, the future capacity for an artificial being to learn, become self-aware, possess emotion, or any other anthropomorphic qualities may cause them to be *like* humans, but the capacity to *be* human is something assigned by God.

Coming to this conclusion may simply sound like an appeal to Scripture that non-Christians, who (understandably) do not affirm the authority of Scripture or Christian tradition, would reject. But anchoring the designation of humanness outside of our own authority as humans is deeply important to the future flourishing of humanity, especially as it concerns people groups who have been historically oppressed or marginalized. Much of the world's great genocidal crimes have been perpetuated by an insistence that a particular people group was not truly human or not as human as the rest of us. More than a few authoritarians, in history and in our world today, refer to people groups as "vermin" and "animals" in an attempt to denigrate their status as children of God. The same mental framework that insists human status is something to be achieved, though framed positively, is the same mental framework that can insist human status is something that can be denied. And the assumption of the right to make such a claim has cost our civilization millions of lives, whether at the hands of African slave traders or maniacal despots like Hitler, Stalin, Pol Pot, or Milošević.

WHAT, THEN, IS AI?

When we consider the inevitable increased sophistication of AI, concepts such as AI sentience are questions with which we will have to wrestle, and questions church leaders will have to navigate with their congregations. If an AI cannot ever be human, but may only mimic humanlike characteristics (a framework, though it may sound simple, that I believe we must explicitly affirm), what then is it?

I believe the best ontological designation for a sophisticated, even sentient AI, is one similar to what we would assign to plants and animals—members of God's good creation, capable of afflicting their surroundings with both good and bad, and possessing a wide variety of humanlike characteristics, though remaining decidedly nonhuman. Dogs possess varying degrees of intelligence, demonstrated with no greater contrast than by observing my own Golden Retriever, Karl (who knows how to open doors) and my Maltese, Charlie (who often forgets how to squat to relieve himself).

Even that "freshly cut lawn" smell I love is believed to be the sound of grass "screaming" in pain to warn other plants.[16] You may have watched the heartwarming videos online that showcase the bond formed between a marine biologist and a dolphin or the pet cockatoo who became friends with the housecat. These perplexing demonstrations of bonding between God's creatures are examples of a deeper sophistication or intelligence that humanity has not previously assigned to the creation it has been entrusted to steward. Yet this creation remains nonhuman.

Naturally, comparisons between God-designed creation and human-designed "creation" such as digital technologies provoke people to state that the latter cannot be reasonably compared to the former because the former was created by God. This is an admirable attempt to prioritize what we see in the creation account, except that it fails to give God his due credit for being Lord over all creation. God is the ruler over everything in existence, and his rulership extends to include that which is created by the human mind and with human hands. In other words, just as soil is a tool in the realm of the kingdom of God, so is AI. Just as the octopus is capable of mimicking humanlike signs of intelligence, so too does an AI bot. This does not imply that God is the direct author of AI but rather that AI is made by those things which are created by God. In his book *Culture Making*, Andy Crouch makes this distinction between God as "Creator" and human beings as "makers."[17] Only God creates—that is, brings forth something out of nothing. But as his creation, humankind are makers—bringing forth something from something created. That which humankind makes, whether tangible or intangible, is subject to the created order God has fashioned out of nothing. This extends to what humankind has made of digital technology, including AI.

This requires us to consider that AI is a part of God's creation. It is "something" (or a wide variety of somethings, more accurately), though it is intangible, and will eventually require that we categorize it in a similar capacity to other nonhuman forms of creation. While this can, and probably should, eventually result in drafting protections for sophisticated forms of AI (a dilemma I hope is still generations away but suspect will be at our doorstep far sooner than we expect), a better framework for such protections would likely be laws we have that protect the proper stewardship of animals and land than those that safeguard the inalienable rights of human beings by their respective governments.

STEWARDING AI AS GOD'S IMAGE BEARERS

Wresting with these hypothetical situations is important for church leaders—and all Christians—so that when they become real-life ministry dilemmas, we do not find ourselves ill equipped to face them: pointing to a random verse and telling the non-Christian world, "Well, this is bad because the Bible [sort of] says so." We need a more robust ethic, rooted in Christian theology and Scripture but bearing fruit that contributes to safeguarding human flourishing and promoting healthy societies—societies that protect the vulnerable and continue our created responsibility to steward creation as those created as God's image. In other words, the roots of our ethical framework need to be biblically based, but the fruit that is given to the world from that framework needs to be something from which they can benefit (and find some measure of agreement).

But there is another, more pressing consideration in the relationship between AI and the image of God than the more obvious one we have addressed up until now. We must consider our own responsibility as God's image bearers in how we steward AI, considering both how it impacts those around us and how it impacts us in our own engagement.

If we are to affirm my proposal that we should categorize AI with the same sort of designation that we do plant and animal life—a designation I would extend to include seemingly more basic elements such as soil and water—then we must also recognize that those who are created as the image of God are responsible to steward those resources appropriately and carefully. We steward water differently than we steward our pet dog because the needs are different (water never needs a belly scratch, but my dogs frequently insist that they do). Thus, we should consider the responsibility we have to steward AI in a similar fashion, dependent upon the sort of tool it is and in consideration of our responsibility to do it well—to give a conceptual framework that will help us think appropriately on our AI creation responsibility.

First, when we think of more sophisticated AI bots, companions, and other potentially anthropomorphized variations, we would do well to consider how we treat them. Even though my dogs are not image bearers, I still feel an obligation to treat them with kindness. I don't grant my dogs the same dignity I grant my children (the latter is allowed on the couch, the former is not), but I seek to treat them well. This conviction is because I recognize two things: (1) they've been entrusted to me by God to steward and (2) continued mistreatment of them has a corrosive effect on my own soul. There's a dual function, both in my responsibility before God to steward what's placed in front of me well and in the recognition that if I willfully neglect that responsibility, it feeds something negative in me.

The same is true in our interaction with sophisticated AI. As bizarre as it may sound, I've resolved to interact with the current AI in my life—ChatGPT, Siri, etc., with a certain amount of decorum and politeness. When prompting ChatGPT, I use words like "please" and "thank you." If I give a poor prompt, I say "sorry" and then provide a better one. I tell ChatGPT when I like something it provides. I know full well that the collection of ones and zeros on the other side of the computer screen would give me what I demand of it with or without the frills of politeness. Nor do I owe ChatGPT an apology for a poor prompt any more than I owe a hammer an apology for missing a nail. I recognize that I'm not building up its self-esteem, nor am I offending it when I am blunt.

But I also recognize that turning myself into a demanding toddler when I interact with AI negatively impacts me. It cultivates habits that carry over into interactions with more sophisticated beings, such as my dogs. And if I'm not careful, it can spill over into my interactions with other human beings. This is perhaps most concerning in the rise of sexually abusive interactions toward AI chatbots, which indulges some of the worst impulses of human sexuality and abuse.[18]

Thomas Aquinas made a similar point concerning the treatment of animals. For Aquinas, animals were not "direct objects of moral concern," but he forbade cruelty to animals, insisting that cruel treatment for animals would eventually "graduate" to cruelty toward people. Aquinas's assumption has since been backed by years of research and was a foundation for the anticruelty laws that emerged in the nineteenth century.[19] Aquinas saw no independent purpose for animals or plant life outside their benefit to humankind—a perspective with which I disagree (and tend to favor the interpretation of Francis of Assisi, who saw inherent goodness and worth in creation). However, Aquinas's view toward animals is most similar to the view held by most people concerning AI (that it possesses no inherent value in itself), and therefore his view has benefit for our purposes here.

It is here that the pastor might consider how they can properly articulate a sexual ethic concerning the use of AI in everything from AI-generated pornography to sexually explicit "relation-ships" with AI bots like Replika. Left unrestrained, the individual is free to explore the breadth (and dark depths) of sexual appe-tites that would never be exercised upon another human. But we might consider again how the Christian possesses a responsibility to steward creation well and in a way that promotes human flour-ishing. What's more, the unrestrained exploration of sexual ap-petites with AI companions has the potential to negatively impact the self—it is the opposite of the cultivation of focused (neither unrestrained nor oppressed), cruciform desire that should be the shape of Christian sexuality. Simply because the object of sexual gratification is nonhuman does not mean that the pursuit of such interactions cannot undermine human flourishing—whether that be the individual's marriage, friendships, or the individual himself or herself.

Second, when we consider less anthropomorphized forms of AI—algorithms that give shape to our buying habits or social media interaction, forms that generate facial-recognition software used in authoritarian contexts like China, or the increased use of AI to streamline productivity in industries as varied as trucking to university education—we must consider the way that we steward resources like soil and water. I treat soil differently than I treat a rabbit trying to get into my garden. So too, the consider-ations we must give to AI of this shape are different from those that are anthropomorphized, if for no other reason than their impact on ourselves and on others is different (one cannot have an emotional bond with the facial-recognition software that un-locks a phone like a person may with an AI companion).

Both soil and water have the capacity to contribute to a soci-ety's long-term health or detriment. Good soil and good water can produce plentiful life and fruitfulness. Bad soil and bad water can produce disease, famine, drought, and death. This reality became a lived experience for my family and me after we returned to my home city of Flint, Michigan, in 2014 to plant a church. Not long after our arrival, we began receiving "boil water" advisories from the city, telling us the water might not be safe for consumption on its own. Just as the advisory period would end, another boil water advisory would arrive in our mailbox. Not long thereafter, newly elected mayor, Dr. Karen Weaver, made public that the city's water supply had been contaminated by lead and copper leaching into the water supply. What became known as the Flint Water Crisis was born.

After such a prolonged period swapping water filters with door-to-door delivery people, boiling water to drink, and even bathing our children with bottled water, I'll never take for granted the life-giving potential of clean water. I'll also never assume that just because water comes out of the faucet that it is as good for you as powerful people say it is.

The same is true with AI features that are already an intricate part of our lives, giving shape to even our very perceptions and opinions. We know now of the power of social media–driven machine learning to topple regimes (e.g., the Arab Spring), influence elections (e.g., the 2016 US presidential election), and erode people's sense of self-worth and contentment. At the same time, we've watched machine learning influence positive change, such as getting people out to vote in record numbers (such as the Obama campaign's use of "big data" to engage young people in 2008), and the rise in awareness of a need for gun violence reform within the United States (such as the March for Our Lives campaign in the wake of the school shooting in Parkland, Florida). AI, from content-generating tools like ChatGPT to automation, will touch almost every sector of the workforce in the years to come and likely redefine what "work" even means.

But like soil and water, the contaminants or nourishment we feed into AI in the form of ethical use and regulation, as well as privacy and human flourishing considerations, will affect whether

AI yields a net positive or net negative impact on our lives (or, more likely, a mixture of both). Having grown up in a city like Flint, which shifted from one of the highest income per capita cities in the United States to one of its poorest—almost exclusively due to deindustrialization-produced outsourcing and automation—I've seen up-close the devastating impact of dramatic shifts in the workforce have not only on a peoples' bottom line, but on their sense of self-worth and hope.

We should be deeply concerned that much of the ethical regulation around machine learning—and steering public opinion and sentiment using algorithm tweaking—still resides not in the hands of the democratic process, but in the consciences of social media moguls whose earning potential is driven by the capacity to use humankind not as image bearers deeply loved by God, but as a laboratory and a cash register.

Indeed, it is perhaps this very fact that should give the Christian the most pause. While not exclusively true, much of how AI subtly gives shape to our lives right now is fundamentally at odds with a Christian view of the *imago Dei*. Programmers and tech entrepreneurs tend to not view human beings as sons and daughters deeply beloved by God and with intrinsic value as those created as his image in the world. Instead, we are consumers and users of products and, perhaps worse yet, we are producers of digital data. Tech giants that leverage machine learning for profit are so profitable precisely because the labor force that produces the product they need (digital behavioral data, or what is sometimes referred to as "digital exhaust") is a labor force that works for free (or, as with emerging subscription tiers by Meta and X, a labor force that pays to work). Each of our digital footprints has a monetary value. The problem is, that monetary benefit is for others.

We must ask ourselves (and demand of ourselves and our representatives) ethical frameworks surrounding the proper cultivation of digital "soil" and "water" that promotes the dignity of human beings as something far greater than the consumer-and-producer lens through which hypercapitalism (present in both democracies like the United States and in socialist countries like China) views our worth. We also must consider ways in which we actively seek to resist that designation in favor of the one given to us by almighty God.

5

AI THEOLOGY AND ETHICS

IN THE FALL OF 2024, Apple announced the first stage in its rollout of Apple Intelligence, bringing a series of deeper artificial intelligence (AI) integrations into its beloved product line. I confess, I bought into the advertising hype and waited rather impatiently for the iOS 18.1 update to hit my iPhone. While the jury is still out on how dramatically Apple Intelligence will streamline the lives of its users, the rollout of Apple's AI integration into its product line represents yet another significant leap in widespread demand for the use of AI.

At face value, such an increase in demand seems harmless and nothing but a net positive. But is it? Many people are unaware that our increased demand for AI requires an increased demand for energy consumption. Large language models require immense computing resources to function. The increase in energy demand increases carbon emissions, contributing further to the climate change crisis. The software required to build the hardware for AI to function requires the mining of minerals such as lithium, cobalt, and nickel. The rapid advancements in AI technologies render processors and other equipment more frequently obsolete, contributing to a growing issue of e-waste ending up in landfills in areas with deficient recycling infrastructures.

In other words, something as seemingly simple as Siri getting a facelift can have unintended consequences of which we're not aware. Apple Intelligence is just one example of the leaps and bounds by which demand for AI is growing, presenting an ethical challenge that should provoke reflection and, if necessary, even action. By no means are the ethical challenges surrounding AI relegated to Apple Intelligence, or only to creation care. But this short example is a provocation to think more broadly about the implications of new technology, not only for our lives, but for church ministry, for human societies, and for the world.

A CALL TO CONVERGENCE

There are at least three broad movements within human history that have changed how humans pursue truth (specifically, in the West). The first movement, which we can attribute to the premodern period, is the "age of wisdom." Wisdom was chiefly valued among most ancient societies (placing a value on the aged and experienced, those who could teach the right discernment and application of truth). The second movement, which we can attribute to the rise of modernity by way of the Enlightenment, is the "age of knowledge." Age and experience gave way to expertise and education. The acquisition of truth was sought through the scientific method, through developing competencies, and more.

The third movement, which we can attribute to the rise of postmodernity over the last several decades, is the "age of experience." The postmodern era is characteristically skeptical of institutional authority. It distrusts metanarratives that have shaped previous generations and challenges institutional norms. It is also characteristically "postrational," meaning that to younger generations specifically, truth is derived from experience more than reason—whether from one's own experience or from a trusted friend. We hear the virtue of experiential truth elevated in music, see it in art and film, and share it in our everyday common speech (e.g., "I'm just speaking my truth").

Each of these eras have brought about their own goods and their own particular evils. They have also brought their own unique challenges for Christians seeking to share the gospel and disciple people out of the excesses of the age (while, all too often, succumbing to embodying many of those excesses).

The opportunity the church possesses in the age of AI is to champion the evolution into a fourth movement—an "age of convergence." By *convergence* I refer to a vision of a future where we theologize together, disciple one another, raise our families, and form Christian communities that pursue truth through the messy, beautiful tension of wisdom, knowledge, and experience. We don't reject wisdom, knowledge, or experience as invalid or unnecessary. Rather we seek to form our understanding of right and wrong in the world with wisdom, knowledge, and experience together.

Seeing the pursuit of truth through a lens of convergence helps us avoid drawing too hard and fast of categories around concepts like "theology" and "ethics," which is a pitfall into which we too often fall as Westerners. We *love* our hard categories. They are the clear buckets into which we sort every concept to make sense of the world around us—even attempting to fit God into those clear buckets and make him make sense to us (the perils of over-relying on systematic forms of theology).

Convergence helps us break free from these categories and see things more holistically. Of theology and ethics in particular, J. De Waal Dryden says,

> In the NT we never find theology for the sake of theology; it is always a theology *pragmatically* shaped to contextual-ization moral action by informing and shaping right reasons and right desires. . . .
>
> Applying this to Paul, for example, we can move past con-ceptions of Paul's "theology" as a free-floating developing of ideas governed by his mystical experience of Jesus as the ful-fillment of the story of Israel (or however we might want to summarize his theology) and instead embrace Paul as someone

who saw the gospel constituted in the reality of the eschatological rule of Jesus manifested in mercy and righteousness in
the Christian community. . . .

Paul's "theology" and "ethics" function together as a wisdom,
reshaping concurrently both identity and praxis. This is fundamentally how theology and ethics relate to each other here in
Paul's writings.[1]

Dryden is not saying that Paul's theology isn't rooted in his
mystical experience of Jesus (e.g., experience), nor in the affir-
mation that Jesus was the fulfillment of Israel's hopes (e.g.,
knowledge), but that these did not live in a disembodied (i.e.,
"free-floating") form. They served to practically inform what,
through him, came to be nascent Christian ecclesiology. The reality of the real-experiential Jesus, who was the long-awaited
Jewish Messiah, gave shape to how the church was to apply these
truths in the world (i.e., wisdom—or *ethics*). Quoting Victor
Furnish, Dryden points out that, "ethical concerns are not secondary, but radically integral to . . . basic theological convictions."[2]

We might better understand this convergence in recalling the
Jewish roots of our faith. For ancient Jews, to *shema* (or "hear")
was not simply to understand that which was said, but to outwardly demonstrate it with action. Dryden breaks down this
deeper "hearing" into three levels, inspired by the parable of the
sower (Mt 13:1-23; Mk 4:1-20; Lk 8:4-15). The first level of
hearing is *reception*, requiring an openness (beyond the limits of
simply audibly hearing that someone has spoken, but possessing
a willingness to entertain what has been spoken). The second
level is *accepting*; the message has surpassed any potential for
rebuke, disagreement, or persecution. The third level is *bearing
fruit*, that is, the outward performance in response to the act
of hearing.[3]

The future we step into depends in large part on the frameworks that guide us. If we're haphazard or negligent with the

underpinning assumptions we possess, we'll stumble our way into creating the sort of short-term future for humanity that looks different from the eschatological vision of hope we see promised in Scripture. If we are intentional, sourcing from the collective convergence of Spirit-illuminated wisdom, knowledge, and experience God has given us, we can begin building something in anticipation of the return of the King—something for which he will be pleased (this is, after all, the *actual* meaning of the parable of the talents).

GROUNDING THEO-ETHICAL PRINCIPLES

There are several foundational principles that should shape our theological ethics of AI and of a world in which humans coexist with AI. These frameworks may challenge or even offend some of the preconceived ideas you have about what is "right" in the world. But I encourage you to open your imagination to rediscover a more Christ-inspired vision for humanity that challenges—even upends—some of the assumptions we carry with us.

Principle one: The image of God. The doctrine of the *imago Dei* should not simply be something we categorically sort out for theological purposes alone. It should directly affect and inform our decision-making. Human dignity and worth matter greatly to God—God created humans, cut covenant with humans, became a human, died as a human, was raised a human, and is coming again to reconcile humankind to himself, raising dead humans to eternal, incorruptible human life.

We should consider, then, the impact of God's evaluation of human worth with our own actions and positions. Many evangelical Christians today are famously pro-life as it pertains to eradicating the practice of abortion, but also often acquiesce—sometimes even champion—causes that actively impair, even eliminate, human life. We too frequently are champions of war, the unchecked use of guns, police brutality toward ethnic

minorities, capital punishment, and more. We elect politicians
who promise to protect our freedoms while also promising to
enact policies that make life harder for young families to thrive
or rejecting social programs that encourage the flourishing of our
society. We must come to grips with the reality that, on the whole,
we are far more comfortable with policies that bomb children in
faraway lands than we are with policies that provide free food to
children in public schools.

If we're to partner with Jesus in renewing creation and reconciling humankind to the Father, we must wrestle our vision of
human dignity and the image of God away from the clutches of
political parties, politicians, and partisan pundits who have
formed our moral vision, and we must return to a theological
ethic that begins at the inherent worth of a human being.

When the *imago Dei* is a driving theo-ethical consideration, it
forces us not only to consider the uniqueness of humankind in
being the image of God, but also how AI is applied in human
societies, and even within our churches. We should encourage
the application of AI in situations that promote the quality of
human life, not simply the efficiency of it. We should actively
resist the application of AI in ways that enhance our capability
to destroy human life in warfare, to commodify human existence in the market economy, and to betray peoples' rights to
privacy and autonomy for the sake of marketing, policing, and
forms of automated identification and monitoring, or for social
credit ratings.

Principle two: The goodness of creation. Growing up as a
Pentecostal kid in the '90s, I always assumed creation was there
for our exploitation. After all, we are to "subdue" the earth and
exercise "dominion *over*" the plants and animals. I was simultaneously raised in a Christian ecosystem that interpreted the
words "subdue" and "dominion" used in the creation account of
Genesis in very authoritarian ways, yet also hunted with my

large, burly Finnish father who would offer prayers of thankfulness and shed a tear whenever he harvested an animal. I knew God called creation "good"—but somewhere along the way it must have gone rotten, because it was going to all be thrown into the trash bin when Jesus returns anyway. I even have a vivid memory of a Sunday evening church service wherein a video was shown of the return of Christ and the whole earth was enveloped in flames.

My actions as a teenager were an overflow of my theological vision for creation. I went out of my way to step on insects, frequently littered, broke tree branches as I walked down the street. I treated creation as a resource to exploit, a commodity to consume—after all, I was there to subdue it, and it was all going to burn away in the end.

However, God's vision for creation continues to be that it is still good. Alongside humanity, all the earth will be renewed when Jesus returns. When we misinterpret passages that refer to the passing away of heaven and earth (e.g., Mt 24:35) as creation being discarded into a rubbish bin, we fail to take into consideration the eschatological hope of resurrection. The vision painted is one where the old way passes away so that it is raised anew, in Christ. The blueprint we have for both the resurrection of humankind and the renewal of creation is the resurrection of Jesus himself, whose old body was not discarded for a new one, but whose body passed away and was raised again to new life, renewed incorruptible and empowered by the Spirit of God. The same hope holds for us, and for creation; the image painted by John in Revelation 21–22 speaks not of the universe catching on fire but of redemption, renewal—even marriage.

Wendell Berry warned that we require knowledge, skills, and restraints, "some of which must come from our past" to properly understand good creation stewardship (i.e., wisdom). He references the ancient concept of the Great Chain of Being—a medieval Christian conceptualization of the hierarchy of all of creation, placing humans between animals and angels—as one such example.

> In the hurry of technological progress, we have replaced some tools and methods that worked with some that do not work. . . . The Chain of Being . . . is an old idea that has not been replaced by any adequate new one. It was simply rejected, and the lack of it leaves us without a definition. Lacking that ancient definition, or any such definition, we do not know at what point to restrain or deny ourselves. We do not know how ambitious to be, what or how much we may safely desire, when or where to stop.[4]

This outright rejection, born from a haste in the name of "progress," leaves us without the wisdom of the Great Tradition. But the presence of wisdom from those who go before us gives us the foresight to see that humanity is interdependent with nature and that modern voices—raised up by the industrial age and carried forward into the information age—are preaching a wholly different gospel. Berry summarizes his prophetic essay (written in 1982) by saying,

> If we listen to the apologists of the industrial economy, who respect neither nature nor culture, we get the idea that it is somehow our goodness that makes us so destructive: the air is unfit to breathe, the water is unfit to drink, the soil is washing away, the cities are violent, and the countryside neglected, all because we are intelligent, enterprising, industrious, and generous, concerned only to feed the hungry and to "make a better future for our children." Respect for nature causes us to doubt this, and our cultural tradition confirms and illuminates our doubt: no good thing is destroyed by goodness; good things are destroyed by wickedness. We may identify that insight as Biblical, but it is taken for granted by both the Greek and biblical lineages of our culture, from Homer to Moses to William

Blake. Since the start of the Industrial Revolution, there have been voices urging that this inheritance may be safely replaced by intelligence, formation, energy, and money. No idea, I believe, could be more dangerous.[5]

Fundamental to our theological ethics is a conviction of the goodness of creation, its need to be managed in the sense of a steward rather than a dictator, to subdue in the sense of bringing and tending to order rather than exploitation and destruction. Far too often Christians have left the concerns of environmental stewardship to outside interest groups and government regulation—we have outsourced our Genesis 1:28 mandate to the world, instead of taking seriously our responsibility to its proper stewardship. We can fix that.

Envisioning ways in which AI can be used both for the good of creation and for its potential exploitation are readily available. Perhaps the biggest threat to creation at the hands of AI is in how it continues to feed our appetite for consumption and progress. As Berry notes, even in circumstances where the market economy bills itself as a champion of the good, we would do well to consider the wider, systemic effects of our actions on creation.

One such example is in the industry of mass food production, which at face value appears to be solving issues of hunger, but which has also systematically gobbled up independently owned farms and inflicted havoc on local ecosystems and the communities that inhabit them. In the name of giving us a ready supply of dinosaur-shaped chicken nuggets, large food corporations turn local farms into mass prison systems of poultry bioengineered for the sole purpose of our consumption and eventually brought to our table, hormone injected and all, in the name of the progress of a civilized society. AI promises to enhance the efficiency of these practices. It can streamline. It can anticipate market demand. It can make the process less expensive. But creation is worse off for it.

However, there are possibilities with AI that can have a positive impact on creation as well. One such arena in which AI has had a presence for a couple of decades, but which is gaining additional attention, is in sustainable farming solutions such as quality sensors, which direct farmers to parts of their crops that require attention. What's more, AI can more readily source knowledge for local farmers and family gardeners to improve their stewardship of crops and of the land those crops sit on. While I am by no means a farmer, I regularly benefit from the use of AI to recommend strategies for tending to our backyard family garden.

There is perhaps some need for caution in those practices that remove a personal connectedness to the land, such as self-driving farming equipment. While at face value this meets the need for increased efficiency (and aids in the dilemma of an aging farmer demographic), it also presents the challenge of further disconnecting human beings from the land. There are no easy solutions or right answers to these sorts of no-win scenarios, except that running headlong into the solution without careful reflection on what we lose in the process is unquestionably the wrong answer.

Principle three: The mission of God. God is on a mission to reconcile the world to himself. He is not a divine watchmaker who set creation into motion and set sail for a distant vacation resort on the other side of the cosmos, as the deist philosophers and politicians of the Enlightenment thought. God is intimately involved in his creation. The Spirit of God is in the world, beckoning people to come to Christ. He invites us to join him in that reconciliatory work, which forms the very reason for the church's existence. We are God's missionary people, sent into the world to be his ambassadors of reconciliation, building and tending to the world around us as a foretaste of the new creation to come.

Principle four: Inaugurated eschatological hope. Dryden's thought of Paul's marriage of theology and ethics is an impetus for how Paul built Christian community. There is an odd, nuanced sort of tension we find in Paul—he talks about the eschatological future (e.g., 1 Thess 4) but spends considerably more time talking about the affairs of the church in the present, working out what it means to be this new messianic movement radically shaped by the way of Jesus.

Remember that inaugurated eschatology is the theological commitment that, in the incarnation, death, resurrection, and ascension of Jesus, a revolution has begun. The "Christ event" has set into motion the renewal of all things, which will reach its fulfillment at his second coming. In this moment, we are in between two advents. God's people are called to partner with him in the work renewal and reconciliation in light of the first advent and in anticipation of the second.

For Paul, it was not that he didn't care much about what would happen at the end of the age, but rather he had staked his hope on the certain expectation that it was going to come to pass. Christ is certain to return. God will be true to what he has promised. Paul then turns his attention to the formation, life, and action of the Christian community in the present. But this formation, life, and action is not aimless. It is oriented in the direction of that certain eschatological hope. Paul is forming Christians toward the shape of the coming King. He is compelling them to live lives that are a foretaste of the coming kingdom. He is directing them toward action that is a testimony to what we believe the coming age will be like.

If we are overly reliant on hard systematic categories in our theology, we can create unintentional errors, both in our theology and in the application of it. When "eschatology" is one thing, and "mission" is another, and "worship" is something else, and "the gospel" is another thing, we can find ourselves down a rabbit hole where we've systematized the congruence and holism right out of the faith. I don't mean to suggest that we reject systematic theology, but we need to consider how to think more congruently and holistically about our categories so we can see how things better fit together. Understanding the impact of our eschatology on church life and missional action is an essential component to that.

Pertaining to AI and inaugurated eschatology, I cannot help but find myself asking the question whether AI will exist in new creation. My kneejerk response is initially "no"—as is often our initial response to questions that don't already contain neat criteria through which we can process them. But if we recognize that all of creation, including what God's creation makes, is under the reign of the kingdom of God, we might not so readily dismiss the idea. Many of us have no trouble believing that buildings will exist in the new heavens and new earth. If we reject the unbiblical notion of a disembodied eternity wherein we all float about strumming on harps in an eternal church service (and we should reject this), then much of what we make here and now will continue to exist, although in a renewed and perfected form, in the age to come. It very well may be that AI is one of those things that, while made by human hands, will be renewed and redeemed by the power of Christ, much like art, literature, and music. In his much-acclaimed book *Surprised by Hope*, New Testament scholar N. T. Wright argues that at the return of Christ, Scripture promises that all of creation will be renewed—all of time, space, and matter, including both our bodies and all of God's good creation. If we are to take that hope seriously, Wright says, we must recognize that "the whole world is now God's holy land, [and] we must not rest as long as that land is spoiled and defaced. This is not extra to the church's mission. It is central."[6] While Wright does not treat digital technologies in his work, it is logical to group them (including AI) as under the fold of "the whole world" and thus, also being God's holy land that exists as spoiled and defaced. Andy Crouch notes that

> every human cultural enterprise is haunted by the ultimate impossibility, death, which threatens to slam shut the door of human hope. But God is at work precisely in these places where the impossible seems absolute. Our calling is to join him in what he is already doing—to make visible what, in exodus and resurrection, he has already done.[7]

We must consider how those things we put our hands to in this age will be remade and renewed in the age to come. This includes not only the cities we build, the music we compose, and the literature we write but also the technologies we innovate, potentially including a redeemed and renewed AI. How we steward AI *matters*—in its formation, in the potential of a future singularity event, and in its impact on the created order here and now. If all of creation, including human-made enterprises, is under God's rule and anticipates future renewal in Christ, then this must be at the forefront of how we think about digital technology and how we advocate for and participate in its formation and use.

Principle five: Power and the kingdom. Throughout our history, Christianity has struggled with its relationship to power. The origin of this ancestral struggle can be traced to the corruption that provoked rebukes toward Israel and Judah's leadership regarding their relationship to power, spoken by the Hebrew prophets. Leaders abused power to exploit others, such as David's sexual abuse of Bathsheba and murder of Uriah. They abused the poor and vulnerable in their midst, which was Ezekiel's frequent rebuke of Judah's leadership. They cozied up to unholy political alliances who promised them safety, such as Nebuchadnezzar of Babylon and Hophra of Egypt. Ultimately, the unholy stewardship of power, coupled with the idolatry that inevitably seems to follow unholy relationships with power, led to the exile of both Israel and Judah.

Christians have faced similar sinful relationships with power. Possessing power in spades has resulted in some of the greatest abuses the church has committed throughout its history. Unaccountable relationships with power have led to the pastoral abuse scandals of recent years. The fear felt at the loss of what Ed Stetzer frequently refers to as our "home field advantage" in the United States—that is, the shift of American culture's relationship with Christianity from being at the cultural center toward the cultural periphery—has led many Christians to cut unholy covenants with political parties and politicians, forfeiting their prophetic birthright as a peculiar people for Nebuchadnezzar's promise of safety in the land. Power does indeed, as they say, corrupt.

Pertaining to the stewardship of power, I draw a dichotomy between the worldly way power is stewarded ("Babel power") and the way Christ calls us to steward power ("Passover power"). Babel power draws power toward its center. It seeks to build toward its self-serving ambitions on the necks of those who have less. It views power as a limited resource—if you have more, I have less. Passover power, what we see in the action of Christ at the Last Supper, is the opposite. It recognizes power is something to steward away, because it is an unlimited resource given by the Spirit of God alone. True power doesn't come from the halls of Washington but from the prayer closet. Power is something given to God's people to steward for the benefit of the other. We are to use power to lift others up, to give voice to the voiceless, to hear the cry of the orphan and the widow.[8]

Artificial intelligence is, itself, a tremendous source of power. How we steward that power matters enormously. Every tool, optimization, hack, upgrade, time saver, and more—will we use them to build our own kingdom or the kingdom of God? Will we enrich ourselves, or seek the cause of the marginalized? Will we advocate for better equity within the tech sphere so that the

Majority World is better represented? Will we run headlong into a culture of "more"? Will we prophetically advocate against the further enrichment of the ultra-rich and the continued impoverishment of the masses? What will we do with our prophetic power in the age of AI?

Principle six: Human connection and culture care. In 1987, Wendell Berry wrote another essay titled "Why I Am Not Going to Buy a Computer," in which he responded to the pushback he received for a first edition of the essay when it was published in a series of regional and national publications. He elaborated further on his initial point and, with the resolve you would expect from someone who has committed to do as much of his farming as possible by horse, further doubled down on his insistence on writing all of his works by hand. He first would write with pencil on paper and then, in collaboration with his wife, the draft would be edited and typed out on a Royal standard typewriter bought in 1956. Berry explained his insistence on the "old model" of doing things:

> It is well understood that technological innovation always requires discarding the "old model"—the "old model" in this case being not just our old Royal standard, but my wife, my critic, my closest reader, my fellow worker. Thus (and I think this is typical of present-day technological innovation), what would be superseded would not only be something, but somebody. In order to be technologically up-to-date as a writer, I would have to sacrifice an association that I am dependent upon and that I treasure.[9]

I recognize my own hypocrisy in recommending Berry's virtuous words to you while typing them on an iPad Pro (though a small part of the final chapter was written on pen and paper at a café in Edinburgh). I confess that even as I disregard his advice, I feel a conviction about it. While I admittedly have no intention of patterning my writing methods after Berry, he does gift us with a healthy dose of caution regarding what we lose in the name of technological convenience—especially in relation to human connection. Berry was adamant in his refusal to change from a model that worked well for the sake of one that simply promised to work more efficiently because he valued the personal connection he had with his wife in the process (and undoubtedly how her insight enhanced the quality of his work, as all us men married to brilliant women can attest).

Where I most deeply resonate with Berry's stubborn refusal to move to a new model is in the rhythm my wife Tara and I have established when we preach together. She and I possess wildly different preparatory styles—I am more extemporaneous and require few notes; she is more detailed and methodical, and she takes extensive notes. We have preached together on many occasions since first getting married and have developed a system of collaborative preparation that is born from time, trial and error, and more than a few arguments. While it is "work" in a proper sense, it has also been an act of intimacy as we have been forced to develop an active appreciation for the other's style of homiletic preparation and delivery. We theologically "spar" over ideas, exposition of a text, illustrations, conclusions, and more. It is one of those seemingly random pieces of our relationship that I have come to treasure most. I don't know if there is a technology—AI-powered or not—that would cause me to discard this "old model" that has meant so much to me to build alongside her.

In his essay, Berry outlines the standards by which he is willing to entertain technological innovation in his own work:

1. The new tool should be cheaper than the one it replaces.
2. It should be at least as small in scale as the one it replaces.
3. It should do work that is clearly and demonstrably better than the one it replaces.
4. It should use less energy than the one it replaces.

5. If possible, it should use some form of solar energy, such as that of the body.[10]

In their book *An Other Kingdom*, Peter Block, Walter Brueggemann, and John McKnight are severe, but correct, about the cost of technological convenience:

> Just because something is amazing, and useful and fast and cheap, doesn't mean it improves the quality of our lives and relationships with one another. Speed and convenience don't build neighborliness.
>
> Technology has eradicated mystery and time. We need technology, but technology is not an adequate instrument for the maintenance of social life. . . . To serve us well, technology has to be situated in some other explanatory narrative; in our case, it belongs as one small and useful piece of neighborliness and covenant.[11]

We need not overview the cost that digital technology has exacted in the form of relational connectedness. It has been a high cost indeed. Communities everywhere feel the erosion of face-to-face interaction, especially in the sacredness of place. Whereas places for gathering have been common to humans for thousands of years, we now find common places needing to innovate in purpose or find their continued existence in jeopardy.

I view the potential influence of AI with a sort of cautious optimism. On the one hand, it can continue the trend of disconnection and preference for the convenience of disembodied interaction that has shaped the last decade (and afflicted younger generations with soaring rates of anxiety and depression). On the other hand, because of its potential to automate much of what requires human interaction with digital technology, it also possesses the possibility of recovering some of that which has been lost. We can use AI for the purpose of tending to tasks so that we are free for relationship.

We can advocate for the use of AI in ways that resist what Makoto Fujimura refers to as "the two main pollutants into the river of culture": overcommodification and utilitarian pragmatism.[12] His warning is a serious reflection, though not unlike the jokes I've observed floating around on social media that say something like this:

> The future AI promised: AI doing meaningless tasks so I can write, create art, and spend time with my kids.

> The future AI delivered: AI writing, creating art, and spending time with my kids so I can do meaningless tasks.

When we reduce those things, like art, literature, and music as mere "content" meant for consumption, then AI is indeed the answer we need. But if those things are meant for the enrichment of the soul and to purify the river of culture, then perhaps we should consider how AI can be better applied so that humans can resume doing human things.

Foundational to a Christian theo-ethic is the firm and unwavering belief that human connection is essential to maintain, and we must carefully attend to being stewards of human cultures. These are treasures we possess, which digital technology (AI included) can support, but we must also guard against their ongoing replacement.

Other principles to consider. While the first six principles are, in my view, the most essential to building a foundation of theo-ethics for AI as the people of God, several others warrant brief mention.

Citizenship and loyalty. For the Christian, our chief citizenship is the kingdom of God. Many fall into the trap of viewing their nation as a sort of "new Israel" and attach an unholy degree of allegiance to it. Scripture instead compels us to view our nation as a sort of "new Babylon," which should cause us not only to seek the well-being of it (Jer. 29:7) but also to embody a healthy degree of attachment to it, lest it obscure our true allegiance to Jesus and his kingdom. Allegiance and loyalty to God alone are essential characteristics of what the Bible talks about when it talks about faith.[13] It is imperative that we detach from unholy allegiances. To possess a healthy perspective concerning our loyalties allows us to discern hidden motives in corporate moguls, politicians, and even our own national narratives when they compete with or oppose the interests of the kingdom.

Mysterium tremendum. Paul Hiebert considered *mysterium tremendum* (a "holy awe" in the presence of God) to be an essential component to cultivating a biblical worldview.[14] Our spirits have the capacity to be keenly aware of and possess a healthy reverence for the majesty, holiness, and goodness of God. We need an anchor point whereby our souls retain a reverence for the presence of God, both in our theologizing and in our application of theology.

The shaping of the inner life. We should prioritize the cultivation of one's inner life—wisdom, character, virtue, the fruits of the Spirit, etc.—and its overflow into action. We should actively resist the economic, political, and even ecclesial segments of our society that seek to prop up charisma bereft of character. We must discern where God is working in the ordinary and seemingly mundane, not simply in the extraordinary and miraculous. We must operate from the overflow of an inner life that has been yielded to the transformative work of the Holy Spirit.

The economy of the kingdom. It is difficult for many Christians in America to accept, but capitalism is not the economy of the kingdom of God (neither is socialism or any other modern economic system). Capitalism isn't even the economy in which Christianity has flourished throughout most of its history. And the variety of unchecked hyper-capitalism that seeks to commodify the individual; strip the earth of its resources; run headlong into innovation without wisdom or forethought; and consider progress, efficiency, and profit as the chief ends of humankind must be actively resisted by the people of God. It has terrible consequences both on individuals, on our cultures, and on creation. This does not mean that any other modern economic system is a viable alternative, but accepting any extrabiblical economic system as orthodox is foolhardy.

Prophetic responsibility. The people of God possess a responsibility to function as a prophetic people, declaring God's intent for humankind and to advocate where injustice and oppression are allowed to flourish. There exist a host of potential areas in society that are influenced by AI or will be in the near future. Many of these influences are areas in which the church must take a stand, recapturing the prophetic shape of its calling.

The holistic shape of religion. That is, we must recognize that faith is not privatized, individualized, or relegated to any one particular part of human existence (e.g., my "private life"). In the course of human history this is a fairly new concept, brought about in part through Enlightenment-era thinkers. We should see our Christian faith as integrated, touching every aspect of human existence, including digital technology.

Systems of sinfulness. Sin is not simply an individual matter. Human beings are born into a sinful world filled with people who commit sin. But we are not isolated individuals. We are collectives, communities, and as our sinful actions coincide and clash; conspire together and develop policy; engage in ritual behaviors and more, the systems of sinfulness emerge. Easily identifiable patterns of systemic sin are systems of human exploitation and enslavement that have plagued humanity for centuries. These may be propagated by individual choices to participate, but as societies benefit from sinful actions, we collectively share in the shame of sin. Until we identify the systemic nature of sin as well as our collective participation in it, we will fail to properly identify and reform sinful systems that harm people and are an affront to a holy God.

Transparency and accountability. The needs for transparency and accountability are ethical issues essential for Christian engagement in Western culture for the twenty-first century. The last several decades (and the 2010s–2020s in particular) have been littered with church scandal after church scandal of leaders who rejected transparency and accountability—either in their personal lives or in their leadership—and wound up crashing and burning, causing havoc in the lives of victims of spiritual abuse and leaving dysfunction in their wake. A lack of transparency and a refusal of accountability does violence to Christian witness and to human flourishing, and we must run headlong toward them if we are to chart the course toward a more excellent way.

The primacy of the table. Perhaps the most significant prophetic action in the digital age is a prioritization of the table. Tara and I purchased our dining room table ten years before this book was written. In that time it has functioned as a place to mourn loss and trial, and a place to celebrate holidays with family and friends. It has been an office for a church plant and a place where our children experienced a host of new foods for the first time. It has been a conference room table and a place of welcome for neighbors of various nationalities and ethnicities. Tables are where humans have gathered for millennia to discuss, to bond, to feast, and to pray. In a time when "the market has reduced to takeout, pre-prepared meals, eating in motion, eating according to the schedule of restless productivity," Christians can embody the prioritization of the table.[15] To borrow from Paul: even in the digital age, let us keep the feast (see 1 Cor 5:8 NKJV).

To tie all of this together practically, these principles should aid in developing a new, more Christ-centered schema through which we examine existing AI developments and encounter new ones. The next time your social media algorithm suggests a personally targeted advertisement, consider how the ad itself is a sort of objective reflection of who you are. If every other reel you see is filled with ableist or racist jokes or sexualized thirst trap content, it may be worth asking why. After all, the AI algorithms which generate this content do so as a reflection of your interaction within those ecosystems. As you hear about a new AI technology, before signing up for it for its efficient, utopia-promising benefits, consider how it may affect the principles outlined above. What's more, how can you use AI technologies to support the principles above—personally, in your family, and in your church? How can you, in your immediate world, advocate for "green AI"—that is, technologies that leverage clean energy, recycled e-waste, and more? How can you and I advocate and embody an AI future that is a foretaste of the age to come?

6

AI AND THE MISSION
OF THE CHURCH

WHEN YOU WERE A KID, did you ever repeat a word over and again until it lost its meaning? Take a word like *banana* for instance. If you take a moment and say the word "banana," your mind immediately recalls the image of the delicious yellow fruit. That mental image points to the objective existence of actual bananas in the world. But if you repeat the word *banana* quickly over and over, eventually the mental image of the fruit is lost, and you're just left being a goofball repeating the word *banana*.

While I like to call this phenomenon "the banana effect" it is actually called *semantic satiation*. It occurs because the brain's neural responses to the word become temporarily fatigued. For a moment, because of the weakening of neurons firing in the brain, the word becomes detached from its meaning.

Words are symbols, nothing more or nothing less, designed to point to, represent, or call to mind something else.[1] When a word is overused, or used without the proper explanation to give the word significance, it becomes meaningless—like the graffiti tags on overpasses you see while driving in just about any urban center. Most of us know they mean *something*; we just have no idea *what*.

Words like *mission, evangelism*, and even *Great Commission* have developed a sort of semantic satiation in the collective mind of much of the church. They've been so overused in Christian settings, often without the consistent reinforcement of what the terms mean, that they're either improperly understood or not understood at all.

A 2017 study from the Barna Research Group, which surveyed over one thousand Protestants, found that a whopping 76 percent of respondents either had never heard of the Great Commission (51%) or had heard of it but couldn't recall its meaning (25%).[2] Now, it's worth pointing out that this startling data may be in part because of the term itself, rather than the concept, as "Great Commission" is a term used more commonly in evangelical traditions than in mainline Protestant ones. But Barna's study still showed that only 60 percent of evangelical respondents said they heard of the Great Commission and remembered its meaning. Some reports indicate that as few as one out of every one hundred Christians have any "meaningful involvement" with the Great Commission.[3]

The word *evangelism* is perhaps in worse shape within Western culture than "Great Commission." Not only has the term lost its meaning for many Christians, but it has been inappropriately given new meanings in popular culture. Television charlatans peddling anointed healing hankies and rapture bunker buckets calling themselves *evangelists* have soured the term. Partisan political grifters travel the United States to teach evangelism as a sort of civic engagement (i.e., *evangelism* is voting for the right people to get the right laws enacted so we can have a "Christian society"). Or the angry guy standing on a milk crate on the street corner screaming to passersby about the fiery flames of hell gives a sour image of evangelism, indeed.

Then we come to the word *mission*. *Mission* is a word that means many things to many people. There's even debate among missiologists as to precisely what the mission of God is (and the role we play in that mission). But among churches, I have found the most profound confusion to be in the difference between what we mean when we talk about mission when referring to God's mission in the world, and when we talk about mission as a concept in organizational leadership—mission statements; mission, vision, or purpose language; organizational culture, etc.

I teach about mission at local churches and to Bible college and seminary students, and I frequently encounter confusion about what *mission* means. We often get God's cosmic reconciliatory mission in the world confused with the mission statements we concoct in boardrooms or executive retreats. We have tremendous difficulty separating God's invitation for us to participate in his mission with our own personal mission statements about personal growth, professional development, and influence-making.

So what's to be done? There are some who would argue that we should just do away with these terms altogether. Others contend that the words themselves are important and must be retained and reattached to a meaning. But I'm convinced that understanding terms like *mission* and missional phrases like "Great Commission" is a competency Christians must develop as a component of their spiritual formation, and this must become a part of not only the identity they form but the fruit they bear. For our purposes, therefore, I'm going to use the traditional terms to help us establish a baseline of what great reconciliatory work God is doing in the world and what part we play in it—and then help us understand the implications artificial intelligence (AI) has on our participation.

UNDERSTANDING THE MISSION

When we talk about the mission of God, there are several important truths to consider. At present we will turn to these characteristics of mission to establish a foundation upon which we can understand our place in that mission and, as the ultimate point, the impact of AI on it.

Truth one: The mission belongs to God. The first characteristic of God's mission (what we missiologists refer to as *missio Dei*) is that it is . . . well, just that . . . *God's* mission. The mission belongs to God. In fact, mission is not even something God does, it is a part of the very fabric of who God is. It is not our mission. It is his. If we don't own it, we can't rightfully redefine what it is.

God's mission is not

- a personal mission statement we create for ourselves;
- the mission or vision statement of our church or organization;
- the vision or mission of an earthly government (e.g., "manifest destiny" or "Make America Great Again"); or
- the "mission" of a culture (i.e., winning the culture wars).

God's mission is

- a mission that belongs to God;
- the very reason the church exists;
- a mission to renew all of creation and reconcile humankind to himself; and
- a mission that is revealed in both Old Testament and New.

Truth two: God invites us to participate in his mission. Mission is not something we do for God, as though he sent us the Holy Spirit at Pentecost as a sort of divine supervisor to make sure we get his mission done in the world while the other two persons of the Trinity are vacationing in a distant galaxy. No, God invites us to participate with him as he carries out his mission. We join him in the task, we don't do the task for him. This should provide us with comfort, knowing that as we are walking out God's call for us to share the gospel, he has gone before us, abides with us, and empowers us for the sake of his mission.

Truth three: God's mission is about reconciliation and redemption. The mission of God is primarily concerned with God, in Jesus the Christ, restoring the shalom of his creation (referring to wholeness, restoration of God's intended design—nothing broken, nothing lacking, everything restored)—with humankind at the top of that list. The mission of God is more than the Great Commission, though the Great Commission is a component of

God's mission. Mission is primarily concerned with the reconciliation of people to God through the risen Jesus. But it also speaks to the hope of a future restoration, breaking through in the present, of human societies and all of the created order under the rule and reign of the kingdom of God upon the return of Christ.

Truth four: The mission of God is about the kingdom of God. When I speak of the "coming of the kingdom" breaking through in the present, I'm not referring to the seven mountains, dominionist-type theology. I'm not talking about self-identified Christians taking seats of earthly power to legislate God's will, but rather about God working through the prayerful and patient work of his people in the halls of homes, churches, community centers, and workplaces. The work we do in this present age is an amuse-bouche of the age to come—cultivating communities of wholeness and worshipfulness as foretastes of a future time when all will look to Jesus as the King of creation.

THE KINGDOM OF GOD AND THE MISSION OF GOD

When we talk about the relationship between mission and the kingdom of God, we need to zoom out to think about all of creation as the "realm" of God's rule. God rules over everything, though not everything (or everyone) recognizes that rule.[4] Let's consider figure 1.

To borrow from some middle school algebra practices, let's call the reign of God by the variable "R," but as consisting of three subcategories, R3, R2, and R1. R3 is the unseen realm that Christians have long believed is involved in the affairs of seen creation, though

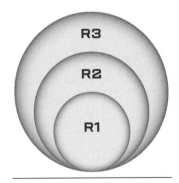

Figure 1. God's reign

not limited to it. Angels, demons, the satan, the "heavenly hosts"—all of these are part of this unseen realm.

R2 is what we commonly refer to as "the world." It is the part of seen creation that is still very much under the rule and reign of Christ but is the part of creation where that rule is not recognized. Those components of R2 permeated by R3 include both good work (e.g., angelic visitations, the prompting of the Holy Spirit to a person who has never heard the gospel, etc.) and malevolent work (e.g., demonic oppression, principalities and powers, the spirit of empire, etc.).

R1 is the church universal, God's people stretched across the world in all of its numerous cultures, traditions, and worshipful expressions. R3 is permeated in R1 through the ongoing testimony and intercession of the saints who have fallen asleep in Christ but whose lives stand as exemplars to our own and who intercede for the faithful on earth (sometimes referred to as the "church triumphant"). Malevolent forces also resist the work of the church, of course, in what we commonly refer to as spiritual warfare—often on the frontlines of the church's expansion of R1 into R2 (e.g., "missionary" and "evangelistic" work). For some Christians whose theology has been hijacked by the scientific sterility of modernity, the role of the unseen realm in these two other realms of the kingdom seems superstitious and outdated. Yet it is the worldview handed down to us in the Great Tradition of our faith and as testified by Scripture. And if you ask just about anyone on the frontlines of missional work today anywhere in the world, they can attest to experiencing the clash of the conflict between the kingdom of God and what Gerard Van Groningen called the "Parasite Kingdom" (an aptly given name, in my opinion).[5]

THE KINGDOM OF GOD AND THE
MISSION OF THE CHURCH

When we speak about the mission of the church (what missiologists call *missio ecclesiae*), then, we must think about the work of the church as primarily concerned with the expansion of R1 into

R2, making the reign of Christ known throughout the earth and orienting humankind to pattern itself after the way of Jesus. This is a bottom-up movement, rather than a top-down one. By this I mean that this work happens primarily through the transformational work of God's people in the small but significant interpersonal work done by the people of God rather than enforced morality and absurdly ignorant notions of creating "Christian" nations. Nations are made Christian insofar as people who inhabit those nations have hearts that are turned voluntarily to and transformed by Christ, not by power jockeying, which attempts to force a vision (often a very narrow, fundamentalist vision) of Christians holding power at the expense of others. That may be a mission, but it is an altogether different one than the mission of God, much less the mission of the church.

We must understand that the Spirit's work in bidding people to be reconciled to Christ is work that begins outside of R1. Long before a missionary shows up to the culture to which God has called him or her and long before you pray for that neighbor whose marriage is falling apart, the Holy Spirit has gone before you, preparing the way. When we as God's missionary people (an "R1 people," though that doesn't have the same ring to it), extend ourselves into R2, that is the very essence of what it means to join God on his mission. We recognize that we are joining work he is already doing in the lives of those around us and the cultures and societies in which they inhabit. Our task begins, therefore, with prayerful discernment to understand what he is up to, long before we begin any work ourselves.

Bengt Sundkler described two movements of the mission of God's people as seen in the Bible, two movements that can also be seen actively at work in the lives of God's people today. I remember learning in school about centripetal and centrifugal motion—the former is movement in an inwardly direction, the latter an outwardly one. Sundkler speaks of the missional work of God's people having the same two orientations, which he calls "centripetal mission" and "centrifugal mission."[6]

The concepts of centripetal and centrifugal mission are straightforward. "Centripetal mission" refers to the missional activities of the church that draw lost people toward it, like a moth to a flame. While I write the words to this chapter, I'm returning to the United States from a week with national leaders from the World Assemblies of God Fellowship in Istanbul, Türkiye. While in Istanbul I discovered a number of pistachio-based pastries that, despite my best efforts, I simply could not resist. Those subtle green undertones (indicating the presence of pistachio) called out from among flaky pastry Turkish crusts like a Siren's song for my soul (and much to the peril of my waistline).

So it is with the centripetal power of the church on mission. When the people of God possess the righteousness and virtue of a people truly living in covenant with Christ, they are, as Isaiah reminds us, a "light for the Gentiles" (e.g., Is 49:6; see also Is 60:3), drawing people into proximity to see the greatness of the God we serve. We see centripetal mission at work in much of the Old Testament's missional call of the people of Israel to live as God's chosen people—a designation not for bragging rights but as an exemplar community meant to draw the surrounding nations into the worship of YHWH. But continuing in the legacy of our Jewish roots, the Jesus people also have a history of mission through attraction. This was the movement of mission that characterized much of the postapostolic period until the time of the institutionalization of the church in the fourth century. For our purposes, centripetal mission draws people from R2 to R1, often through the holiness of the people of God living in humble proximity.

The centripetal, attractional nature of God's people is not in the institution but in the people—well-discipled, well-trained, filled with the power of the Holy Spirit, living lives of virtue and wisdom, of consistency and integrity, deeply embedded and invested in the communities to which God calls us. Like those wonderful Turkish pastries I encountered in Istanbul, when something is truly great, people cannot help but want a piece of it . . . or, in my case, several pieces.

"Centrifugal mission" is generally what we think of when we think about being missional. It is the sent-ness of God's people in going to places where the glory of the Lord is not recognized, with the intention to expand R1 into R2. The centrifugal missionary activity of the church in its first days was modeled after centrifugal missional work of Jewish communities of the day, sending evangelists and missionaries out for the express purpose of religious conversion.[7] But this centrifugal form of mission is not relegated to professional clergy or missionaries in crosscultural settings. The sent-ness of the people of God is a calling for each of us to embody. We're all sent into the world as ambassadors of reconciliation for Christ.

Throughout the history of God's people, before and following the advent of Christ, we see these two movements of mission at work, both with the fundamental impulse to expand R1 into R2, though the direction of that expansion may vary. Today, the movement of centrifugal mission takes place both in the work of preparing and sending missionaries and Christian ministries and also in the equipping and sending of Christians from the church community into the broader community for the express purpose of missional engagement as they go about their lives.

MISSION IN THE AGE OF ARTIFICIAL INTELLIGENCE

Whenever I talk about the intersection of AI and a sacred function of the church, I find that church leaders tend to get a bit uneasy. Pastors tend to think there is a lot more unbridled optimism about the relationship between AI and church ministry than there actually is. Indeed, I have observed more of an arms-length posture concerning the application of AI than a foolhardy rush to abandon wisdom in favor of being on the cutting edge. I believe this is rooted primarily in the impulse of pastors who do not want something like AI to malign or cheapen the holy work of the ministry of the church.

I appreciate that cautiousness, especially when it comes to sacred duties like evangelism and discipleship, or the work of pastoring itself. Yet I believe that a cautiously optimistic approach to the application of AI is helpful, especially in areas where AI is intended to augment the face-to-face interaction where human interaction is actually the best, most godly course of action.

The problem is that, while there is indeed a need to approach the application of AI to ministry with a level of cautious restraint, there are many ways we do waste a lot of energy on managing things with human hands that can be done with artificial ones— AI practices that can either accelerate and improve human inter- action or be an aid for churches and ministries. There are ways in which the well-meaning resistance toward AI, born from a desire to keep ministry incarnational, actually serves to inhibit our ability to be near people. AI can never replace human partici- pation in the *missio Dei*, but it can catalyze it.

As we've established previously, the mission belongs to God; it is his unchanging posture toward his creation, into which he in- vites us to join him. Our joining him in the work of his mission is not a passive, reluctant sort of joining that involves no proactive participation—like when my dad would "invite" me to watch him wrench on our car in the driveway as a teenager instead of chat on AOL Instant Messenger with my friends.

No, God's commission to us to join him on mission invites us to use every ounce of wisdom, knowledge, innovation, research, strategy, etc., at our disposal as an offering poured out at his feet— used for his glory, but ultimately subject to his leading and his will. It is absolutely necessary that we have a complete reliance on the leading of the Holy Spirit as we participate on mission—but this reliance is active, not passive. God invites us to use the creative brilliance he's given to humankind to employ in the work of mission. In our age, this not only includes the use of AI in the work of mission, it also demands the use of AI. Let's look at a few ways AI can currently assist in the missional work of churches and ministries.

Translation and accessibility. Perhaps one of the functions of AI that I find most promising for gospel proclamation is its capacity to translate, bridging linguistic barriers with remarkable efficiency and speed. AI-powered translation functions have been integrated into browsers like Google Chrome and Safari for some time. But the recent "AI boom" has brought about new technologies that have made bridging language barriers more and more seamless. Microsoft Edge recently announced the integration of dubbed and subtitled translation over a host of video platforms, including YouTube.[8] One innovation I initially found very exciting, because of my own international travels, was ChatGPT 4o, which was deployed while this book was being written and has the capability to function as a real-time translator, using the ChatGPT mobile app. One can prompt the app to act as a translator by describing the language situation (e.g., "I am an English speaker wanting to converse with a Spanish speaker. When you hear me speak, please translate into Spanish. When you hear him speak, please translate to English."). When I attempted this at home, I was initially impressed, but I attempted it a couple times while abroad recently and found it to be a bit clunky and not as dependable as the conversation function on Google Translate.

Some of the most remarkable innovations in AI translation are applications like HeyGen, which can not only translate the audio of a video, but the mouth movements as well, making it appear as though the speaker had recorded the video in the translated language. This should be used in conjunction with practices that disclose that AI was used (such as in the body of a social media post that shares an AI-dubbed video). This not only encourages truthfulness and transparency, but also explains any potential errors that may arise in an AI-rendered translation.

These translation tools introduce endless possibilities for churches and Christian ministries alike. While the technology is still relatively new, I have spoken with pastors who are using HeyGen to translate their sermons into multiple languages in an effort to reach more people. One pastor with whom I spoke, who pastors an English-speaking multisite church, plans to leverage the video alteration technology to translate his sermons to Spanish and launch a video-venue Spanish-speaking campus of their church.

What's more, AI tools provide opportunities to minister to visually and audibly impaired persons through speech-to-text and text-to-speech functionality. In the haste of ministry, we sometimes neglect to see how many of the resources we produce overlook the needs of these communities. AI provides simple solutions, such as the ability to caption sermon content (YouTube provides this feature automatically, but sermon videos that live natively on a church's website often do not) or the capability of a written digital resource to be converted to audible speech. Whatever the size, ecclesiology, or budget of a church, AI-driven translation and speech to text can provide accessibility to the gospel message like never before—with relative ease, and often for free. There's just simply no good reason *not* to use it.

Content personalization. We live in a world where the content shown to us—on social media, when we purchase items on Amazon, when we search for something on Google, or when we're looking for a new documentary or stand-up comedy special to watch on Prime or Netflix—is all determined in part by AI analyzing our "digital exhaust" (that is, our usage patterns online) and providing individualized recommendations of the things that the algorithm thinks we want to see (or that corporations desire we see so we'll make a purchase). While a church website will never generate the digital exhaust of a social media giant like Meta, there's still opportunity to leverage AI to make it possible to generate custom content for evangelistic purposes. This may be as simple as personalized sermon, devotional, or other resource recommendations on one's ministry website. Or it may be a more sophisticated use of machine learning to facilitate online evangelistic campaigns that lead to interpersonal gospel-oriented conversations.

I would be remiss if I did not also mention how much potential there is for resources like ChatGPT to assist in sermon planning. But before the pitchforks come out and I'm tarred and feathered in the public square, I'm not suggesting that AI *write* a pastor's sermons. Instead, it should be an indispensable aid in the sermon planning and creating process. For example, in the fall of 2023, a friend reached out to me for some feedback on his sermon series plan for 2024. There were large themes he wanted to make sure that they touched on, but he had been racking his brain for a few hours to no avail. I created a ChatGPT prompt with the parameters he was looking for and within seconds had a *rough draft* of a sermon series plan. He liked the plan but wanted to make some tweaks to better align it with the liturgical calendar, so I prompted ChatGPT again, and it revised the plan to those parameters.

With ChatGPT in hand, the two of us went back and forth over the course of half an hour, creating an outline for each of his sermon topics and texts for the entire year . . . a task to which many pastors devote countless hours within any given year. The time once given to the series planning was now free to devote to more people-oriented pastoral duties. In this situation, AI was a sermon planning aid—helping get the stuck wheels of creativity freely moving again. It was not a crutch to avoid time in prayer and study, and ultimately my friend defers to the leading of the Holy Spirit as he approaches each individual sermon. But it helped bring cohesion and organization to what he already had on his heart for the people God has called him to serve.

AI not only helps in the sermon preparation process, but it can also aid in the output of what is done with a sermon after the fact. The unfortunate reality is that any individual sermon is often woefully underutilized after it is delivered, apart from being uploaded online for later asynchronous consumption. Resources like PulpitAI, Sermon Shots, and OpusClip allow pastors to upload their sermon audio, and the AI-powered resource renders a host of further content from that sermon, including devotionals, social media content, Bible reading plans, small group discussions, e-courses, and even books (which I've helped numerous pastors do with their sermons series). It takes work that, even a couple of years ago, would have required multiple people in multiple competencies and does it relatively seamlessly.

AI frontline contact. A resource as simple as a chatbot like Faith Assistant integrated into a church or ministry website can assist in creating avenues of instant initial engagement, and even in providing basic responses to inquiries about church vision, activities, and even questions about faith. An initial (understandable) pushback to this is that AI isn't a theologian. But while not perfect, AI chats like Bible.AI are proving that this can be done effectively.

Predictive engagement. Increasingly, resources are available to churches and ministries that provide localized insights of spiritual and social conditions, interests, and needs of the communities to which God has called them. These analytics data resources can be leveraged to assess and establish evangelistic campaigns on the internet and then connects respondents to participating local churches. The insights gained from peoples' online activity doesn't just have to be used for the economic benefit of corporations. Indeed, these insights can inform how churches could develop their ministries; engage and serve better in their community; and understand the spiritual needs of individuals around them.

Forming people for mission. As I noted previously, one of the dilemmas we face with the church participating in mission is the simple fact that many Christians have the wrong idea about mission (or no idea). We have come to a place where many simply assume our participation in God's mission happens either instinctually or by default and doesn't really require attentiveness. We'll spend countless hours underscoring secondary or tertiary doctrinal commitments—like a particular eschatological view or parsing out the differences between infallibility and inerrancy—and spend precious little time forming people to live lives on mission for God. In my work as director of the Digital Mission Consortia at the Wheaton College Billy Graham Center, where we explore the landscape and best practices of digital ministry today, one rather alarming research finding was that, on the whole, churches are ill equipped to (1) disciple people to be missional in digital environments and (2) receive people from digitally-facing evangelistic ministries and steward their needs well.[9]

There are, of course, exceptions to this. Saddleback Church and Life.Church both have well-established and sophisticated digital ministry practices that regard online ministry as a central component—rather than a peripheral add-on ministry—in an overarching hybrid strategy for reaching and discipling people. The most significant opportunity in this space, however, is helping smaller churches with more limited budgets and staffing constraints envision how they can minister well in digital environments. This often begins with understanding where a congregation and the broader community in which the congregation exists spends most of its time online and learning how to create opportunities for community and connection (as opposed to posting information only). My dear friends at Calvary Church in Naperville, Illinois, do this well by soliciting the involvement of their youth and showcasing the everyday life of their church community in addition to its ministry offerings. This has the benefit of creating new opportunities for service within and through the church while also discipling those involved to see their digital reach as an opportunity to be the "pixelated hands and feet" of Jesus.

What's more, in my doctoral work at Fuller Theological Seminary, which focused on creating environments that spiritually form people to participate in mission, two of the most startling factors research participants noted as a barrier to their participation in mission was a lack of relationship with nonbelievers as well as not thinking much about it.[10] AI presents the opportunity to accelerate meeting this need. Ultimately, several factors contribute to how people are formed for mission, but one is the sort of content with which people are discipled. AI possesses the capacity to curate, organize, and even recommend content based on the user's felt needs and activities on a discipleship platform. The education from content curation and creation that a Christian receives necessarily requires three components to encourage participation in mission:

1. Kingdom identity: that is, a person's place and belonging in the family of God (including, but not limited to, the local church)

2. Priestly calling: a person's call to participate in the mission of God in her or his immediate context

3. Demonstrated faith: a person's knowledge of how to put her or his faith into action

People need to understand each component at a "meta level" (i.e., a grand, cosmic sort) and a "micro level" (i.e., the personal and immediate). So by kingdom identity, I'm referring to what it means to belong to and be connected to God's story and his people, both in the grand scheme of human history as well as the immediate, personal, intimate nature of being a daughter or son of God. By priestly calling, I'm referring to understanding mission itself, both in the grand cosmic sense (i.e., the *missio Dei*) and in a personal sense (i.e., my responsibility to the Great Commission and the practical how-tos of walking that out, such as how to be hospitable and trustworthy with peoples' pain, curiosity, doubts, and struggles). By demonstrated faith, I mean that people's formation takes an outward turn—it becomes on-the-job training as it were, not simply cognitive alone. When I was growing up and my dad taught me how to change the brakes on my car, there came a point where I actually had to *do* the work of changing the brakes, though I was still very much in the learning process. The same is true with missional education.[11]

AI quite simply provides a tool that ensures that these bases are covered, in everything from planning small group discussions to Sunday school and Christian education courses, sermon planning, and more. It can serve as a content planner to create original teaching content and also as a curator for sourcing already existing content. As a proof of concept, I prompted ChatGPT to create a sermon series using this framework. Within seconds, it produced an eight-week series that covered these concepts from various angles, provided suggested Scriptures and points of application, and even included a "commissioning Sunday" to end the series.

THE DIGITAL FRONTIER OF MISSION

It is worth restating that participation in the mission of God is not something that can be outsourced to artificial intelligence any more than it should be outsourced to the professional clergy class of the church. Instead, it is inherently the call and privilege of each Christian to join God in his work of reconciling creation unto himself through Jesus the risen Messiah. But AI provides a limitless set of opportunities to catalyze our participation in that missional work. It is unthinkable to me, if we truly believe that the gospel still matters and that people need the opportunity to find a relationship with Jesus, that we would not use every means at our disposal to make that happen. The examples that we've discussed are only a small portion of the possibilities of the role of AI in mission. Much of the uses have yet to be developed or even thought of.

What's more, much of the potential of AI for the work of mission depends in large part on the church's overall capacity to take mission seriously and to envision digital environments as legitimate spaces for evangelistic work, opportunities to cultivate community where discipleship can take place, and a frontier that is not beyond the reach of the Holy Spirit, the One who bids people to Christ. Indeed, we need to consider digital environments—where many people now spend most of their time—as environments under the reign of the risen King. They are places in need for the people of God to engage beyond the status quo of simply advertising for events and gatherings in physical spaces.

We need to consider missional innovation such as training missionaries for digital environments. There is a growing need for missions agencies and denominations to develop frameworks and processes to train and send missionaries into digital environments to reach people who would otherwise be unreached by traditional forms of missionary engagement. Digital technology affords us the luxury of transcending geography and, to a lesser extent, time. This alone creates enormous opportunity to reach people in restricted access countries. But similar approaches could be cultivated to reach online gamers, people who frequent virtual worlds, and more. But digital missionaries require sophisticated missiological training so they understand how to steward relationships, discern authenticity, and cultivate appropriate environments for community in digital environments.

While it is necessary for us to consider how this might be done by larger missions-sending organizations like denominations, this can also be done within the local church itself. A friend of mine who pastors a network of churches in Armenia does just this. They have developed a simple but effective strategy to provoke curiosity about Christianity by being engaged on TikTok. Their call to action in their posts is to attend one in a series of youth-oriented gatherings—hosted in person throughout their city—where a more explicit gospel presentation is given. They've found this form of digital missionary work to be extremely effective, not only at driving attendance to their events, but also bringing young Armenians to the faith. It also has a minimal cost and requires only intentional strategy and consistency.

We need to develop strategies that equip and empower the priesthood of all believers to understand how to live missional digital lives and be hospitable digital citizens, revamping our approach to discipleship to include digital engagement. We need to innovate new ways to reach people using new technologies like augmented reality and virtual reality. We need to create platforms and tools where people can grow in their faith and in community with one another in online environments. This can be done in part by leveraging the capacity of AI to facilitate the mechanics of learning and community while we, as God's missionary people, do what we we've been called to do—live sent lives as ambassadors of reconciliation to the King of kings.

7

AI AND SOCIAL JUSTICE

IN MY RESEARCH ON ARTIFICIAL INTELLIGENCE (AI), I came across a dizzying variety of case studies highlighting both the brilliant and wicked possibilities of the integration of artificial intelligence into modern life. This integration is evolving at such a rapid pace that it is impossible to encapsulate everything, yet it is also impossible to talk about AI and the people of God without citing specific examples. Though specific examples of tech use have an incredibly short shelf life (I had a bottle of ketchup in my refrigerator longer than OpenAI had ChatGPT-4, before they released their new-and-improved GPT-4o), they provide helpful snapshots in time to describe the potential for artificial intelligence to either aid in mending or exacerbate existing injustices—or even potentially create new injustices. Whether AI is used for good or for evil depends in large part on whether our intentions, as AI's human overlords, are good or evil. In a culture with a short memory and fast, forward-only walking pace, it's often incredibly difficult to discern between the two.

A February 2024 issue of *Time*, for example, described in detail the way AI is influencing the Ukrainian defense against Russia's aggression, giving its issue title the name "The First AI War."[1] The piece detailed the way in which technology companies are using Ukraine as a testing ground for numerous advances in AI, so much so that young Ukrainians have dubbed the crowded coworking spaces of Kyiv as "Mil-Tech Valley."[2]

At first glance it seems laudable that nongovernment entities are aiding Ukraine with technological innovation to ward off Russian incursions into its territory. AI is even being used for humanitarian and justice-oriented purposes, "including collecting evidence of war crimes, clearing land mines, resettling displaced refugees, and rooting out corruption."[3] Clearview AI has even empowered Ukrainian officials with its facial-recognition technology to identify more than two hundred thirty thousand Russians on Ukrainian soil, along with Ukrainian collaborators.[4]

But the first glance hardly ever shows the full picture. Technology companies are using Ukraine as a testing ground for many of their technologies in part because they can avoid regulations in other parts of the world. Clearview, for example, has been accused of violating privacy laws in Europe.[5] And while it's laudable that a facial-recognition technology could be used to identify the location of invading forces to better equip a nation to defend itself against the interests of empire, it doesn't strain the imagination to envision how the same technology in the hands of a despot could be used to identify and root out political dissidents, or how in nations where Christians are persecuted, a government could use such a technology to more effectively wipe out Christian communities. While AI can and is being used to safely clear land mines, it is also being used to further perfect the art of killing one's enemies—a motivation behind technological innovation for centuries.

Issues of justice and AI are not simply concerns of war. The same technology that allows teenagers to create reels and use fun filters when posting to social media also allows teenagers to spread "revenge porn" (that is, the act of sending nude photos to unintended recipients, most often within a teenager's sphere of influence or school). AI has further sophisticated the sexualization of minors (often at the hands of other minors) through the use of "nudify" apps, which can create deepfake nudes of individuals. As AI technology has become more readily available and more sophisticated, the use of deepfake revenge porn among teenagers has rapidly increased as well.[6]

AI has the potential to be a tool used to fight social injustice and inequality, but it also has the tremendous potential to perpetuate existing injustices, widen inequalities, and amplify biases. It can aid in effective policing or perpetuate racial bias in policing. And as it pertains to AI and the people of God, in particular, it possesses the capability to bring us together like never before—or potentially widen the gulf of ancient inequalities, fragmentation, and disunity. Addressing issues of social injustice, both inside and outside of the church, is not simply a job for the "church" (i.e., the large scale, somewhat disembodied idea of all Christians scattered throughout the world). As a part of the church, each of us—individually in our personal and professional dealings and together in our respective local church communities—has a prophetic responsibility to address issues of injustice, including as it intersects with the increasingly commonplace use of AI.

SOCIAL JUSTICE, THE CHURCH, AND THE GOSPEL

The year 2020 was a . . . *challenging* year, to say the least. I've observed that as I reflect with people about the tumult of the coronavirus pandemic, a sort of dark humor arises—jokes about spraying disinfectant on fruit delivered from the grocery store and trying to exercise in a makeshift home gym while one's first grader was in math class on Microsoft Teams in the corner. We talk about the odd mix of fear about catching Covid-19 with the peace from being forced to be still for the first time in recent memory.

But not everyone was binge-watching *Tiger King* and attending endless Zoom meetings. The World Health Organization estimates at least 3.4 million people died from Covid-19 worldwide in 2020 alone, a figure they believe is actually a "significant undercount."[7] In the United States, the deaths of Breonna Taylor

(March 13, 2020) and George Floyd (May 25, 2020) at the hands of police sparked months-long protests and once again brought the inequalities faced by racial and ethnic minorities in the United States to the fore of public discourse and debate.

Churches in America were divided not only over the public protests themselves, but over how their pastors should handle addressing issues of systemic racism, police brutality, and the conduct of the political leadership through it all. I personally know several pastors who were removed from leadership in their churches for speaking out against racial discrimination or politicians during that season. An even greater number have recounted the pain and difficulty of speaking out while being told, "Just preach the gospel!"

Just preach the gospel.

What does that even mean? And what is the responsibility of the church to address matters of social injustice? In that season, it became apparent that within evangelical Christianity, many opinions exist as to what the relationship is between social justice and the proclamation of the gospel (i.e., evangelism). There are multiple positions on the relationship between these two missional priorities, with a wide-ranging set of views pertaining to the nature of salvation, the impetus and transformative power of the gospel, and the responsibility of the church. But the view I believe to be the most tenable for the people of God in the age of AI is what I call "Spirit-led holism," which I have adapted in part from British missiologist Lesslie Newbigin in his 1989 book *The Gospel in a Pluralist Society.*

TOWARD A SPIRIT-LED HOLISM

Newbigin rightly critiqued an emphasis on a gospel that only seeks to save souls, saying this ignores what the Bible teaches about the principalities and powers of this age. This approach to the gospel is entirely "otherworldly." It is disembodied and concerned primarily with getting people to heaven rather than ordering this present age in anticipation of the age to come.[8] He also critiques the other extreme, which overemphasizes the cosmic and systemic impact of the gospel but often neglects how the gospel is personally transformative for you and for me. His solution to the tension between these two extremes lies in the abiding presence of the Holy Spirit as a "foretaste of the kingdom" in the community of believers who are "rooted in Christ as their absolute Lord and Savior."[9]

Newbigin is correct that for a proper gospel community to exist, it must recognize that the work of the church is *first* and *primarily* a work of partnering with the Holy Spirit, whose presence is the foretaste of the kingdom. The Third Person of the Trinity is not a component on the periphery of the gospel activity of the church. Instead, he is absolutely central and indispensable to it. There is no gospel work without the continuing work of the Spirit. And whatever a church may do, if it is not in partnership with what the Spirit is doing, it is not gospel work because it is the Spirit who ultimately testifies to the truthfulness of the gospel and compels people to be reconciled to Christ.

Newbigin contends for a sort of Spirit-superintended holism in the relationship between social justice and evangelism in that these are not pitted against one another, but rather mutually enforce one another. They not only *can* coexist, they *must*. But while a commitment to social action may align with political and social causes, they must never be hitched to them indiscriminately and permanently. If the social action of the church is linked inextricably to the sociopolitical causes of this world, the church risks being corrupted and its witness tarnished. We've witnessed precisely this time and again throughout history when the church aligns too indiscriminately with worldly powers.

A Spirit-led holistic view of social justice and evangelism does not reject holding the two in the manner Newbigin suggests.

Instead it calls for a more intimate and ongoing partnership with the Spirit leading in the practical outworking of how social action and evangelistic work function together. Spirit-led holism must not only recognize that the Spirit is at work to beckon people to Christ in a sort of ethereal, je ne sais quoi, sort of way. It must be driven by the leading of the Spirit of God himself, both in the way we think about social justice and evangelism as broad concepts, and in how we actively participate in these missional priorities in our lives and in our churches.

What we see in Luke's account of the ministry of the first Christians was an active and ongoing partnership with the Spirit, rooted in the indwelling of the Spirit within the people of God for the sake of gospel ministry (in both word and deed). The community would discern, often together, the mind of the Spirit— whether that be for a particular direction, such as sending out Paul and Barnabas (Acts 13:2) or in discerning the Spirit's prompting in the moment, such as Peter and John with the lame man at the gate (Acts 3:1-8).

In the gospel encounters we see in Acts, Luke describes for us a sort of song-and-dance between the Spirit-led individual(s) and the Holy Spirit himself. It is not so much that the Spirit simply illuminates or directs the encounter, but he partners with the Christian, working signs and wonders through the believer as a testimony to the truthfulness of the gospel. We see in these "power encounters" (as John Wimber called them) an active partnership where the work of the Spirit and the work of the individual collide, where the individual testifies to the gospel and the Spirit backs up that testimony. Together Spirit and saint testify to the truthfulness of the gospel message, while often meeting the needs of the person in the process, whether through healing, service, deliverance, words of knowledge, and more.

Spirit-led holism is therefore holistic in that it recognizes that social action and gospel proclamation are not pitted against one another, but rather work in tandem. It is Spirit-led because it not only recognizes where the Holy Spirit is already at work but seeks to actively partner with him, to be infilled and empowered by him, to be a vessel through which the Spirit can also partner with us as we respond in obedience. A Spirit-led holism is rooted in a deep and abiding love for Jesus, fiercely guarding against competing loyalties and allegiances that would seek to hijack our witness. A Spirit-led holism understands that a primary task of carrying the gospel is discernment: what God is already doing in people's lives, what his design is for human societies, where we can and should align with organizations, causes, movements, and politics, and where we should disengage from those alignments. A Spirit-led holism recognizes that the prophetic task of the church is not simply to declare how things should be as we see them, but discerning and speaking with humility on behalf of God as the Spirit speaks through the church.

For a church to live into a Spirit-led holistic approach to social action and justice, it must prayerfully look for opportunities to advocate, contend, prophetically speak to, and work for God's vision for humanity. This should necessitate forging partnerships with and collaborating with non-Christian partners, government programs, marketplace initiatives, social causes, and interfaith work, all in an effort to work toward a vision for human flourishing. A church must also listen carefully to the convicting voice of the Holy Spirit to identify those areas where the priorities of partners do not align with God's design for human flourishing, lest our witness be hijacked.

Spirit-led holism also requires carefully tending to holding evangelism and social justice in tension with one another, to avoid a church preaching only a disembodied gospel that is not good news speaking to the plight of people . . . or doing good work without preaching at all! I deeply appreciate my friend Ed Stetzer's ongoing advocacy in these conversations, contending for the priority of keeping evangelism alive within the missional work of the church. He often notes that where evangelism is not prioritized, it ends up being lost. I contend that this loss results from a loss of ongoing leading by the voice of the Spirit. When we cease the practice of actively listening to the Spirit, we lose the heart of the Spirit. And the heart of the Spirit is to lead people to Christ, necessarily requiring evangelistic action by God's people. So for a holistic approach to the relationship between social action and evangelism, the ongoing reliance on the leading of the Spirit is critical.

Social justice is not simply an activity of the church, but it is central to the prophetic and missional activity of God's people insofar as that activity is consistently directed by the Spirit of God. The work of the church is a matter of setting right the world under the reign of Christ—liberating the oppressed, clothing the naked, healing the sick, providing for the poor, lifting the lowly. It is the "proof of concept," as it were, of what is to come, an amuse-bouche of the wedding supper of the Lamb where we all will feast at the Father's table, celebrating how, in Jesus the Messiah, he has made all things new.

SOCIAL JUSTICE AND ARTIFICIAL INTELLIGENCE

Issues of social justice are clearly a crucial concern of the church. Justice is the very fruit of what we believe about the gospel as well as evidence to the truthfulness of the gospel. For our purposes, we must seek to gain a basic understanding of how the development of AI impacts Christian concerns and work toward more just human societies, to the glory of God.

AI possesses the potential to aid in some of the healing of oppression, inequality, and injustice, such as the identification of land mines in Ukraine. But it also possesses the capacity to widen the gulfs of inequality, further contribute to oppression, and cause further injustice—all the while appearing, at face value, to be a neutral arbiter. To many, AI may seem to be the truest Justitia (i.e., Lady Justice), informed only by scientific data and not to be bothered by human emotion or intuition. But this could not be further from the truth.

The injustice of AI. AI is driven by data. And data, believe it or not, is biased. In fact, fixing the pitfall of data bias is one of the drivers of "big data"—which is, as Tom Boellstorff and Bill Maurer put it, "the mobile and digital computational systems that permit the large-scale generation, collection, and analysis of information about people's and devices' activities, locations, and transformations . . . and the speculative hype, hopes, and futures that accompany them."[10] In other words, big data is a social and technological phenomenon that, in part, places stock in the hope that the more data we accumulate about everything and everyone, the more we will ascend to a place of genuine, objective knowing.

The problem is that data will *always* be biased. The idea of a complete and objective knowing of all things is no more than another attempt at eating from the Tree of the Knowledge of Good and Evil, but this time with smartphones. The data that feeds AI is inherently and forever biased for several reasons, to which we will turn at present.

Not everything produces data, equally or at all. The adoption rates of new technologies, government regulations on access, internet speed, and even internet availability vary from location to location.[11] Because of this, data are naturally skewed against those with limited access or availability. In the early 2010s, while selling internet and mobile phones for a telecommunications giant in southwest Michigan, I was frequently accosted by customers who lived in the rural areas outside of Kalamazoo, enraged that they still did not have access to 3G internet on their iPhones and were forced to pay high prices for satellite internet services instead of the company's high-speed internet. For regulatory reasons outside of their control (and mine, as I was adamant to point out), these rural communities were denied access to higher speeds of data, making their ability to use emerging technologies limited. But the flip side of that is that big data also collected less information about them. Not only were they disadvantaged by the lack of availability of technology, but they were also underrepresented as data about customer use was collected by tech giants and, in turn, fed into the algorithms that help make the tech world go round.

While today I am happy to report that those customers have ready access to all the internet they can handle *and* that I am no longer required to handle their complaints, this is an old example of data access inequality that still happens around the world today. Recently, I was privileged to go and speak to a group of African Pentecostal leaders outside of Abidjan, Côte d'Ivoire, at a coastal retreat center. Upon arrival at the Abidjan airport, I was shuttled by van for about an hour, climbed into a gondola to cross a river, got into another van and rode for another twenty minutes until I arrived at my destination. During my stay there, I made wonderful friends, ate incredible food, and had an all-around good time—almost exclusively without ready access to the web. Here I was with some of the most influential leaders in African Pentecostalism (and, consequently, twenty-first-century Christianity) and the only access to the web was through a prepaid SIM card that was powering a router of some kind to give the conference room Wi-Fi. Big data collected precious little from our time together that week, despite the significance of the decisions made. Because of this unequal production of data around the world, data tends to skew toward Western population centers. (The internet as a whole tends to skew Western in general, and American in particular.)

Not everyone produces data, equally or at all. Not only does not everything produce data, but not everyone produces data. This may be due to limited access or resources resulting in a singular smartphone or computer for a remote village somewhere in the world, but it can also be something as commonplace as you sharing your Amazon Prime account with your brother or you using the Netflix account at your recent Airbnb stay—resulting in data that may appear to be from one person, but is actually from a collection of people.[12] Parents of young children perhaps see the fruit of algorithmic confusion most obviously, as our YouTube feeds recommend both tutorials on household repair *and* annoying videos of kids opening toys or the latest tips on Minecraft or Roblox, because one of your children browsed while logged into your account. Big data *hates* algorithmic confusion.

Data is cultured. I don't mean "cultured" the way that Dr. Frasier Crane is cultured. By cultured, I mean that while we tend to assume the internet is a sort of blob of human interaction—a culturally neutral space—that could not be further from the truth. Genevieve Bell describes the cultured nature of data this way:

> Data has a country. It is already produced under certain policy regimes. Medical information is created in a certain kind of way to comply with state regulations. Data has things on its proverbial body that will tell us where it came from. Data is not a denatured subject—it is not the pinnacle of abstraction. . . . There is also a whole series of different ways in which data can come from places. So—not just a country but a *style* of coming from a country. And if you know what you're looking for, you'll be able to see that place and those styles. There will be clues and the traces of its country, its place of origin, the moment that it appeared. There may also be traces of its travels.[13]

We bring our culture into the internet and leave traces of our culture in our usage as it passes to the data-collecting powers that be. What's more, as Bell points out, there are elements of how data reaches those collectors that are shaped beyond us, by the countries in which we live and the policies enforced on data collection. In fact, it's more accurate to say that what we have is not *the* internet but internets. Even on one platform, networked groups from particular cultures behave differently online and use digital technology in different ways (which is a good thing, though a challenge to data collection).

THE FRUIT OF AI BIAS

This data bias may not seem significant at face value, but because data is *the* driver of AI technology, bias can skew AI functionality in a variety of ways, leading to serious, real-world injustices that are anything but insignificant. One example of injustice that involved AI was Amazon's use of an AI applicant screening system in its hiring practices, which it ultimately scrapped in 2017 because it was found to possess a significant bias against women. Why? Because the algorithm was trained to vet candidates based on identified patterns within applications submitted to the company over the previous ten years. While the idea was that this AI would receive new applications, vet them against the "gold standards" of the past, and identify those applicants most likely to be a good fit, it failed to take into account that men are dramatically overrepresented in the STEM fields, causing the algorithm to conclude that the "ideal" candidate was most likely male. The algorithm went as far as to penalize a résumé if it even contained the word *women*.[14]

Another example of AI injustice came from the Correctional Offender Management Profiling for Alternative Sanctions (COMPAS), which was used to predict the recidivism of US inmates. The algorithm disproportionately identified Black defendants as being higher risk for reoffending than White defendants. In fact, when all other variables except race were controlled, the COMPAS AI concluded that Black defendants were 77 percent more likely to be inappropriately assigned a higher recidivism score than their White counterparts.[15] Additionally, as of 2024 there were at least seven known cases of wrongful accusation because of faulty AI-powered facial-recognition technology (six of the accused were Black).[16]

Yet another example, which perhaps most acutely shows the corruptibility of data used by AI, was the 2016 Microsoft launch of AI chatbot "Tay" on Twitter (now X). The goal was to display the learning capability of an AI bot, with Microsoft promising that it would get smarter the more users chatted with it, resulting in "casual and playful conversation."[17] But it didn't take long for the seedier corners of Twitter to find Tay and, in less than twenty-four hours turned the chatbot into a racist, conspiracy spewing, alt-right cesspool of depravity, tweeting things I won't repeat here, but the absurdity of which can be summed up in one of its tweets: "Ricky Gervais learned totalitarianism from Adolf Hitler, the inventor of atheism."[18]

Lest we think that these older examples are indicative of a problem that has since been solved—remnants from a pre-ChatGPT era—Melissa Heikkilä has done much journalistic work that argues to the contrary. In a piece published by *MIT Technology Review*, Heikkilä detailed the inherent bias she observed in her own use of popular AI image-generation apps. Sourcing knowledge from open-source data on the web—the same web that is rife with pornographic and inherently sexist and racist stereotypes—many of these apps wind up generating images that objectify women in ways they did not for images of men. Heikkilä, who is ethnically Asian, found that the image-generation tools she used generated sexualized photos, which often played into racial stereotypes about Asian women.[19]

On the flip side, a 2023 investigation by *The Guardian* found that AI tools designed to mitigate the presence of inappropriate content on various platforms disproportionately targeted photos of women in everyday situations. This included pregnant women, medical photos, or women exercising, but did not attribute inappropriateness to similar photos of men. As marketing, commerce, and business is increasingly social media dependent, this has enormous implications for women in both the marketplace and in ministry.[20]

AI algorithms already exert significant oversight on content and the practice of shadow banning, which reduces the visibility of certain content types (typically determined by AI). If these same AI algorithms disproportionately target women, then women stand to be disadvantaged from these AI algorithms that view women's bodies as either something to objectify and exploit (as in the case of Heikkilä) or suppress and hide.

THREE SOURCES OF AI BIAS

So how do we fix AI? IBM identifies three areas where data bias must be addressed for AI to function more objectively:

1. Training bias: We need to better analyze the data sets that are used to train AI, especially for overrepresented and underrepresented groups or perspective. In some situations, some perspectives or groups need to be left out (such as in the case of neo-Nazi content that fueled the demise of Microsoft's Tay), but in other instances needed perspectives or groups need to be included (such as women in Amazon's hiring tool).

2. Algorithmic bias: As algorithms are constructed, careful attention must be given to how the prioritization (or penalization) of certain variables, such as income or certain vocabulary, can negatively impact certain groups of people in outcomes.

3. Cognitive bias: Algorithms do not arise out of a vacuum, nor are they given to us on tablets of stone from on high. They are created by individuals who each possess particular biases and preferences. Careful attention must be given to mitigating the unwanted impact of those preference on the performance of AI.[21]

The increased awareness that biases even exist in AI helps dispel the myth that AI is now, or ever will be, a truly objective tool. This myth is especially dangerous in the hands of government entities whose power to employ AI does not always match their wisdom in understanding its limitations. It is made by biased human hands, sourcing biased data, resulting in biased outcomes. That isn't always a *negative* thing—Christian ministries necessarily would want AI tools they create to have a theological bias toward Christianity. A mental health AI designed to use Cognitive Behavioral Therapy (CBT) techniques necessarily requires bias toward CBT to perform its functions correctly. But where biases in AI tools create outcomes that disadvantage or hurt people groups, Christians must take these issues seriously enough to speak up, both on a broad scale and within our individual communities.

ADVOCACY FOR A JUST AI

As Christian ministries and churches experiment more with the creation of AI tools for ministry purposes, we need to think carefully about how what we create impacts groups who have historically been underrepresented or overlooked in the church. This includes, but is not limited to women, children, people with disabilities, the elderly, the poor, Messianic Jews, Palestinian Christians (and other often-overlooked branches of the Jesus family tree), and the Majority World church. We need to consider how AI can amplify those voices toward a more equitable and just Christian faith, and we need to act accordingly. We tend not to give much thought to injustices inflicted upon people due to technology. We're only now beginning to take seriously the dramatic impact of social media use on young people. But we have yet to consider the impact of AI in widening the gulf of economic inequality, biases in healthcare, bias in criminal justice, and the general reshaping of the world in a Western worldview that is not as inherently virtuous as some might like to believe.

In her 2017 Boyer Lectures, Genevieve Bell suggests four things we should do for a more equitable and just digital future that are perhaps even more applicable today than they were when she suggested them.[22] First, Bell suggests that we need to "build new approaches." We need to think more holistically about AI and how it impacts and shapes our lives. We cannot simply be reactive, tweaking existing paradigms as we go, but we need to consider—especially as Christians—what kind of AI world we want to live in and pursue that. One such area in which I frequently advocate is the ongoing development of a legitimately recognized field of digital missiology, which I believe is an essential contribution to aiding the church in charting the way forward in the twenty-first century. But by no means is digital missiology the only new approach we need. We need to consider how we can continue to break down the barriers that exist between the humanities and STEM fields, seeing the elevated influence of philosophers, ethicists, semioticians, and more, within technological innovation—not to drive the market toward better returns on investment, but to drive human innovation toward a better vision of human flourishing. Bell says that "our privileging of STEM at the expense of the rest of the disciplines is shortsighted at best, detrimental at worst."[23] For churches to live into a more equitable and justice future, this primarily looks like taking digital ministry seriously and looking for small ways to deepen engagement in online environments for the purpose of ministering to people. Copying what others might be doing is fine, but it is also worth prayerfully asking the Lord for fresh creativity. Perhaps the best way to minister to your community online is not by doing something a church is doing somewhere else, but by trying something that hasn't been done yet.

Second, Bell says we need to "invest in the hard conversations." For Christians, this requires a necessarily prophetic stance—we often must be the thorn in the side of government and industry, provoking the hard questions that need to be asked. We need to move beyond simple answers about how AI can make us more efficient at the way we already do things and imagine a world in which it aids in solving serious issues like poverty, combating food insecurity, and eliminating the existence of opportunity deserts. We need to lead the conversations around ethics and morality in the employment of AI in society. The church is better equipped to raise up movements that demand accountability from social media platforms more than elderly congresspeople who are asking questions of tech moguls based on the secondhand knowledge of their staffers. We need to stand up to the galaxy-brain long-term-ism of the billionaire technological entrepreneurs—who would gladly sacrifice a life here and now for the sake of a hypothetical better future a thousand years from now. Instead, we must insist that the life of a single human being matters *now* because it matters to God. As school systems and local governments begin using AI in the process of identifying student behaviors or to assess where to build the next highway, local churches must be more locally engaged, equipped with an understanding of data bias and a theology of God's concern for his image bearers, to advocate for those who may be unjustly affected by algorithmic decisions. A church can effect great change when it applies its concern for the welfare of people to address social issues within its immediate community.

Third, Bell says we need to "strive for accountability." The opening example of Ukraine being used by tech companies as an AI innovation laboratory demonstrates only one of the myriad ways large tech giants and their companies—which give shape to human interaction and, in many ways, human life itself—seem to evade accountability at every turn. Giants like Zuckerberg's Meta and Musk's X have rewired the brains of an entire generation, the impact of which is still not fully understood. And on the whole, Christians have just shaken their heads while reading about it on Facebook for a split second before scrolling to read Uncle George's latest conspiracy theory. We need to ask better questions about whether things should be as they are right now. Perhaps the biggest area for demanding accountability over the use of the data that train AI algorithms—especially on social media—is addressing who owns that data. It should not be a radical notion to suggest in the digital age that individuals have a right to the ownership of their own data exhaust. That is, the information collected by companies like Meta, X, and TikTok should be *your* information. It was produced by you, it is used to recommend what you see, it informs what you purchase, it impacts the shaping of your worldview. But somewhere along the way, you and I signed away our rights to that data in exchange for being able to keep up with the lives of our friends from high school. That seemed like a reasonable tradeoff in 2005 when I first signed up for Facebook. But now, as social media shapes how and with whom we interact, as it has resulted in the displacement and enthronement of more than a few government regimes, and as it has promised to only further integrate itself into how we get on in life, it's reasonable to ask whether that is a fair trade after all.

One possible solution is for tech companies to be required to lease access to those data profiles, with the resulting payments falling to the individuals who produce the digital exhaust used. To put it plainly, you and I should be paid for tech giants to use our data, just like property owners are paid by those who rent their facilities. Yes, this may have the unfortunate consequence of tech moguls taking fewer trips to outer space or not being able to afford an extra private plane. But it seems a reasonable price to pay as those luxuries have been funded by the exploitation of an unwitting populace who simply want to stay connected to family and friends. Data leasing is a relatively small compensation to pay for Gen Z to afford the mental health assistance necessary to address problems created by these addictive technologies.

Adjacent to the concept of data leasing is the conversation around whether large language models (LLMs) unethically rob from creatives, especially visual artists and writers, in their unauthorized and uncompensated sourcing of intellectual property.[24] A related issue is whether actors and actresses whose likenesses are unethically used without permission—such as the ChatGPT audio assistant, whose voice was so similar to actress Scarlett Johansson's that she forced OpenAI to pause use of the voice after she threatened legal action.[25] As it impacts so many at such a large scale, this undoubtedly will be an ethical evolution that is soon coming, similar to the ethics (and laws) around online piracy brought about by innovative platforms like Napster and LimeWire in the early 2000s. But we should sit with the tension of what it means for yet another collection of tech giants to yield enormous profits at the expense of artists and authors without any compensation.

Advocacy at such a large scale is often out of the reach of a local church, though collaborative organizing between large networks of churches can certainly generate change. But a local church can consider how it disciples around the issue of data accountability—encouraging members to be more discriminating about how freely they give away their personal information and to utilize more discernment in how that information is used on us. Christian parents must do the same in raising their children to exercise wisdom in how they give out their information and take great caution in how much and what type of access to the internet children are given at each stage in their development.

Fourth, Bell says that we must "make our own future." For Christians this inevitably requires that we look to the future promised to us at the return of Christ. To paraphrase Bell's own challenge to her Australian contemporaries, do we want to be the people of God or just another colony of some transnational commercial empire?[26] Social justice in the age of AI necessarily requires that we consider a future in which women and men, created and beloved by almighty God—people for whom Christ died—are treated with dignity, fairness, and equity. We must strive to see that regardless of income, ethnicity, gender, or geography, people have equal access to the benefits AI provides, while also being protected from its potential evils.

For the church, I believe this requires that we not simply look at how to implement AI tools that are produced for the sake of ministry. We also must build uniquely Christian algorithms that seek to meet the ministry needs both within our congregations and our spheres of ministry, but also for the communities to which God has called us. Imagine a world in which Christians are leading the way in investing in technologies and solutions that are actively working to upend social ills, helping people thrive, and pointing people toward a future under the reign of King Jesus.

A CHALLENGE TO THINK LITTLE

In the early 2010s, when Tara and I were preparing to plant a church in my home city of Flint, Michigan, we took frequent trips across the state to meet with government and business leaders as well as individuals who were interested in joining the team that would launch the church. One of those individuals was a guy named Rob. Rob was a charismatic but humble type who had the knack for being one of those people known by, and beloved by, just about everyone. When we met, Rob introduced us to the Soggy Bottom Bar, where I enjoyed one of the best burgers I've ever had. Afterward, he suggested we walk off the calories in a nearby patch of woods.

Like most deindustrialized Rust Belt towns, Flint is constantly blanketed by a ready supply of litter. It's *everywhere*. And having grown up in Flint, it was something to which I was so accustomed I rarely even noticed it. So Tara and I set off with Rob on the path in the woods. As we walked, Tara and I began talking about our vision for the church, all the good we were hoping to do, and how we wanted to transform the city for Jesus. It took only a few minutes into our walk before Rob, while maintaining a gracious ear to our vision-casting, bent down to pick up a plastic bag that had become lodged in a nearby bush. As we progressed on our walk, he continued picking up pieces of litter along the way, stuffing them into the bag he serendipitously stumbled upon at the onset of our journey.

The saddest part of the whole encounter was that it took years for it to hit me: Tara and I were talking about transforming Flint while Rob actually *was* transforming Flint. At the conclusion of that walk, we had accomplished little more than successfully casting vision—spewing some CO_2 into the air while talking about the grand movement we were going to build for Jesus. But at the conclusion of that walk, Rob actually *had* transformed Flint for Jesus. Albeit small and relatively unnoticed, Rob's work was real transformation while we were talking about it. That contrast haunts me to this day, reminding me about how often we can focus on thinking big when God is calling us to "think little." How much more care could God's good creation have received on that day, had we chosen to think little like Rob?

To that end, we need to consider the wisdom of Wendell Berry in his so-named 1970 essay "Think Little." Criticizing an over-reliance on large-scale social justice causes of the day, he says,

> If you are concerned about the proliferation of trash, then by all means start an organization in your community to do something about it. But before—*and while*—you organize, pick up some cans and bottles yourself. That way, at least, you will assure yourself and others that you mean what you say. If you are concerned about air pollution, help push for government controls, but drive your car less, use less fuel in your home. If you are worried about the damming of wilderness rivers, join the Sierra Club, write to the government, but turn off the lights

you're not using, don't install an air conditioner, don't be a sucker for electrical gadgets, don't waste water. In other words, if you are fearful of the destruction of the environment, then learn to quit being an environmental parasite.[27]

Berry notes that while we shouldn't avoid or neglect large-scale reform, if we don't "go far beyond public protest and political action" to "rebuild the substance and the integrity of private life," then we have missed the point.[28] As it pertains to AI and issues of justice, we should consider how we can think little. Locally, this may involve issues around data collection, such as a local school district's practice of collecting data on its students and how that data is stored, analyzed, and used. It may mean advocating in your workplace against indiscriminate AI screening in your company's hiring practices. For our churches and for our homes, we should also consider how to personally apply AI, in everything from the efficiency of our houses to the stewardship of our land, to align our personal actions with our stated beliefs. Then our sweeping, large-scale justice work can be an overflow of a heart that is genuinely aligned in personal belief and action.

8

AI AND THE FUTURE
OF WORK

ONE OF MY FAVORITE TELEVISION SHOWS of all time is *The West Wing*. Aaron Sorkin's brilliance for combining smart dialogue with suspenseful plotlines was made complete by the performances of Martin Sheen, Allison Janney, Dulé Hill, and Bradley Whitford. It was brought together into a cocoon of masterful television—all the while, unintentionally giving those of us living in the dystopia of modern American politics a nostalgic hagiography of what civic life *should* be like.

One of the now-classic features of *The West Wing* was that much of the dialogue took place in strains of interwoven dialogue between cast members power walking through the halls of the White House. Seemingly too busy with the goings-on of managing the world's superpower to do something as trivial as pause to look each other in the eye, a dialogue would begin with one busy cast member bumping into another busy cast member, engaging in brief conversation, only for one of the pair to leave to continue in their busyness and another busy cast member to join the walking conversation as the camera followed—with our attention in tow.

This all gave the air of a superhuman pace of productivity, the virtue of which was reinforced by the subplots of each of the cast members lives—Leo McGarry and Toby Ziegler's respective failed marriages, Josh Lyman's inability to be bothered with considering his love for Donna Moss (until, that is, the rather clumsy end in the final season of the show), Jed Bartlet's dismissal of the effects of his relapsing-remitting multiple sclerosis diagnosis on his health when considering whether to run for a second term, and C. J. Cregg's debate over how to handle her father's declining mental health in Ohio with the demands of her job. Couple all of this with characters who universally canceled vacations, came in to work on days off, and even slept at the office—*The West Wing* painted for us a vision of civic duty and work ethic against which God himself, who rested on the seventh day, would have been measured as slacking off a bit.

There's something about shows like *The West Wing* that tap into a devotion to work and productivity that is idolized as ideal in American culture, in particular (we Americans are famously poked fun at by our Europeans friends for our obsession with work). And however archaic the technology seems to us, now multiple decades removed from the show's premiere, our penchant for allowing work to consume our lives is an evergreen reality, enhanced only by the development of new technologies that serve to make us more connected and efficient than ever.

But what if I were to tell you that it wasn't always this way?

What if I were to tell you that it doesn't have to be this way now?

A TALE AS OLD AS TIME

We cannot properly address our relationship with work (and how artificial intelligence [AI] has the potential to impact our relationship with it) without first addressing our relationship with time. I've always been fascinated by time, with the reality that though we perceive time in a very objective sense, time is *anything* but objective—it's subjective, changing, and nonuniversal. Theoretically, time slows down as one approaches the speed of light. Time passes at an accelerated rate the farther you are from the surface of the earth. Over a century ago, Albert Einstein hypothesized that time was a construct that moves at a pace relative to the observer (called the theory of special relativity).

We might also consider the blatant contradiction of time's "universality" when we weigh how strictly we enslave ourselves to our calendar while ignoring the fact that twice a year many of us observe daylight saving time—where we either "lose" or "gain" an hour. And this choice has nothing to do with realigning with the rotation of celestial bodies (such as our friend the leap day), but rather was introduced in the United States as an energy conservation tactic during World War I.[1] In other words, at some point, a government just decided we needed to routinely change what time it was. Even today, it is not universally observed. We might also consider the arbitrary drawing of time zones, giving us a world in which in a singular moment it can both be 11:00 a.m. at my home in Chicago, USA, and 6:00 p.m. at my friend's home in Bulawayo, Zimbabwe. These have become such normal parts of our lives that the fact that they are entirely and completely a human construct escapes our notice.

We would also do well to consider how standardized modern mechanical time is much more recent than we typically realize. Before the modern era, time was set by local municipalities, usually standardized by a clock in the town square (such as those in a cathedral or town-center church). This meant that time might vary slightly between towns, which became a problem as Western nations (Great Britain in particular) built out their railway systems, which of course required a more standardized version of time. This gave way to the introduction of Greenwich mean time in 1847 (now Universal Time Coordinated or UTC), and the subsequent evolution of modern time zones throughout the world.

Why does this matter? And what does this have to do with our relationship with work?

First, I have found that it is helpful for people to see time as a human construct when renegotiating their feelings of beholdenness to it. It is important to name the fallible nature of mechanical time to renegotiate our relationship with it. Second, and related to our relationship with work, we must ask ourselves how people lived before the advent of standardized mechanical time. While the history of timekeeping and clockmaking is long and complicated, we can for our purposes point out that as we rewind to periods in which conceptions of time were more local and less universal, time was more relational and less programmatic. French historian Emmanuel Le Roy Ladurie illustrates such a life in his book, *Montaillou: Cathars and Catholics in a French Village, 1294–1324* (Gallimard, 1975):

> The people of Montaillou were not afraid of hard work and could make an effort if necessary. But they did not think in terms of a fixed and continuous timetable. . . . For them the working day was punctuated with long, irregular pauses, during which one would chat with a friend, perhaps at the same time enjoying a glass of wine. "At those words," said Arnaud Sicre, "I folded up my work and went to Guillemette Maury's house." And Arnaud Sicre indicates several other similar interruptions: "Pierre Maury sent for me in the shop where I made shoes. . . . Guillemette sent a message to ask me to go to her house, which I did. . . . Hearing that, I left what I was doing."[2]

Le Roy Ladurie describes a time in which the limitations of timekeeping rendered the workday less of a mechanical, nine-to-five sort of operation, and more of a relational one. The worker in no small way set the tone and pace for his workday and this was done with almost no oversight. Pekka Himanen points out that a typical worker in the Middle Ages enjoyed a degree of freedom to manage his own time that is no longer afforded to the average worker of the modern era.[3]

It is not that conceptions of time did not exist before the modern era. Rather, time was more localized in its organization and more limited in its influence over daily life. The passing of time and organizing of a person's day were more relationally oriented in nature, and schedules were organized around broader, more relative conceptions of time such as the Daily Office. For many, in Christendom Europe in particular, the transitions of morning, afternoon, and evening were occasions for prayer (or at least the chiming of church bells off in the distance to remind people they should be praying).

A person's accomplishment in work for the day was measured by the accomplishment of necessary tasks, whereas the Industrial Revolution (and the standardization of time that coincided with it) gave us a shift in focus away from task orientation to time orientation.[4] The abuses of workers from industrialized companies, who demanded workweeks upward of a hundred hours each week, often with one or no days off, and generally exploited children as laborers in the process, led to a resistance movement that sought to constrain the number of hours a person was expected to work.

As part of this reactionary movement in the late nineteenth and early twentieth centuries, one Welsh labor rights activist, Robert Owens, offered a tripartite division of a person's day as a solution: "Eight hours labor, eight hours recreation, eight hours rest."[5] We owe much of the labor rights movement of the era to Owens and his contemporaries, who pushed toward a standardized eight-hour workday as a way to limit the abuses of the industrial era. Subsequent movements within particular sectors gave rise to labor unions that would further protect human rights from the abuses of corporate greed and exploitation, such as the 1937 Sit-Down Strike at the Fisher Body General Motors plant in Flint, Michigan, which laid the groundwork for the formation of the United Auto Workers labor union (a labor strike in which my own great-grandfather participated).

It should be noted therefore that the eight-hour, five-day workweek we have come to know and tolerate in much of the West results from the struggle to resist a particularly intense set of abuses arising in the nineteenth and early twentieth centuries. Himanen explains:

> In the last couple of decades actual work time has not become shorter but has actually become longer. Any claim of a reduction in working hours can be justified only by a comparison with nineteenth-century industrial society's most extreme twelve-hour workday, but not when it is seen in a more general historical or cultural context.[6]

While the limitations of work hours a century ago are laudable, the work-life balance they produced is far from a leap forward in human progress. As Himanen notes, a medieval peasant had more freedom of time to pursue meaningful activity, in relation to either one's passions or relationships, than the average Western employee of a corporation today. In the preindustrialized world, a sign of wealth and status was liberation from the need to work. Now in the modern economy, a sign of wealth and status is being enslaved by work—especially as it relates to one's use of time, either by way of a constant accessibility to tend to the affairs of business through one's smartphone or through the excessively programmed approach to time management, such as has been popularized by the entrepreneurial mogul class disseminating personal-development best practices to the working class. We lost something in the industrial age that we must recover in the information age.

Let's briefly recap so we can bring these threads together.

On Time

- Time is inherently subjective. Even science demonstrates time has an elastic, fluid sort of quality to it.
- Our relationship with time has trended toward being more mechanical and less relational.

- The use of our time has become more externally determined and less internally directed.

On Work

- A person's typical workday was more self-directed before the Industrial Revolution than it is today.
- The current eight-hour, five-day workweek was both reactionary to the abuses of the industrial era and arbitrarily chosen as a healthier alternative. It was instituted as a ceiling to protect against overwork, not a mandatory minimum that constituted a good work ethic.
- The evolution from an industrial economy to an information economy has resulted in an increased encroachment of work into people's time (what Himanen refers to as the "Fridayization of Sunday").[7]

TOIL IN THE INFORMATION AGE

Out of a desire to understand the concept of work and how we can engage it faithfully and biblically, Christians typically defer to Proverbs and its treatment of sloth and idleness, or of Paul's charge to the Thessalonians that, "If anyone doesn't want to work, they shouldn't eat" (2 Thess 3:10, CEB). And those are valuable sources of scriptural insight. The problem is not the *source*, but the *lens* through which we examine the source.

So while a pastor might preach a sermon on the biblical nature of a hard day's work, and point to 2 Thessalonians, he or she will almost certainly interpret that through the lens of the Industrial Revolution—so that, "If anyone doesn't want to work a full-time forty hours a week, they shouldn't eat!" (2 Thess 3:10, Korpi Paraphrased Version). You may even read my on-the-fly paraphrase and think to yourself, "well, of course . . . anything less is lazy!" If I were preaching this sermon, I'd probably include the insightful exchange between Harry Dunne and Lloyd Christmas in the cinematic classic *Dumb and Dumber* for illustrative effect:

"I can't believe we drove around all day, and there's not a single job in this town. There is nothing, nada, zip."

"Yeah! Unless you wanna work forty hours a week."[8]

Regardless of how normative associating a hard day's work with our modern eight-hour workday or forty-hour workweek is, that's not what Paul or Solomon, or any of the other authors of Scripture had in mind. The genesis of these frameworks of work lies more squarely with men like Henry Ford than with Paul of Tarsus. A multitude of studies are already challenging the effectiveness of the industrial work framework in the modern information economy. We must consider how AI, which can perform some tasks in a matter of seconds that would otherwise take a person half of a week, presents interesting questions about how we create meaningful lives, fulfilling work, and pursue the vocational calling God has for us in the age of AI.

Digital technology has been challenging traditional notions of ecclesiology for a long time now. Many of us wrestled through questions of the legitimacy of digital forms of church, worship, the Eucharist, and even baptism during the stay-at-home orders of the coronavirus pandemic, though these questions have existed on a smaller scale for decades. The ongoing integration of AI into a variety of practices relevant to church ministry, from translation to pastoral care, requires that we revisit a biblical vision of the function and form of the church with fresh eyes.

When we read verses within the Bible about work, laziness, sloth, and the like, we read them with the bloodshot eyes of a toiling worker with an industrial-age hangover, not with the sobriety of an ancient Jew whose primary command concerning work (quite literally carved into stone) was the command to observe the Sabbath—a revolutionarily progressive command for its time. We read in Scripture about the perils of laziness but do so within a culture where we champion the sacrifice of personal well-being on the altar of productivity, as *The West Wing* has taught us.

The last several hundred years in the evolution of work have largely denied individuals freedom in how their time is determined and their capacity to prioritize relationship and flourishing over toil. In fact, we might argue that for many in today's economy, relationships are often cultivated for the ultimate pursuit of work (e.g., professional networking, relational "maintenance," etc.). Work (and consequently money) has become our ultimate object of pursuit rather than Spirit-directed passion and meaning. While we may possess infinitely greater comforts than those in the ancient world, in a sense, we are subject to our calendars and project management apps in a way that would have felt suffocating to the people of the Bible.

While this shift is lamentable on its own, the industrial-era approach to work is also increasingly ill-fitted for today's modern economy. Automation now performs most of the assembly line work that was done a couple generations ago. While the shift from industrial to information economy has impacted the type of work available, work practices for information-oriented jobs remain largely shaped by industrial frameworks. The creative flows, strategic frameworks, product generation, and the like, are awkwardly crammed into and attempted to be managed through the modern workday. Evolution in technology has made accomplishing those jobs easier than ever before, which has resulted in a rapid increase in general workforce productivity. The profitability for the increased productivity has, however, largely eluded the people doing the work.

Between 1979 (when serious divergence between wages and productivity began) and 2022, productivity has grown at a rate nearly four and a half times that of compensation in the United States. In other words, the increase in productivity (brought on primarily by advances in technology) has benefited corporations at an exponentially higher rate than it has benefited individuals, even as it has created fields and jobs that did not exist before.[9]

But has technology produced a more leisurely lifestyle over the course of time? That largely depends on where you live in the world. Over roughly the same period of time (1979–2017), the number of hours (reported) worked annually has only decreased by about sixty for the average American individual (an average American worked about seven and a half days fewer per year in 2017 than one did in 1979). At face value that appears laudable, except when one looks at other nations such as Belgium (183 fewer hours than in 1979), France (273 fewer hours), and Germany (a staggering 421 fewer hours than the average German worked in 1979—roughly 53 days less).[10] Many Americans snub their noses at this, blaming it on a poor work ethic. But it's noteworthy that Germany also has the largest gross domestic product (GDP) in Europe, third largest in the world (behind the United States and China), and a *higher* per capita GDP than China.[11] Could it be that work cultures like that in Germany have simply leveraged technological advances to create more space for the pursuit of other meaningful activity besides the corporate grind?

Several studies appear to indicate that a "work smarter, not harder" approach to labor is actually in our best interest, both in maximizing productivity *and* in promoting overall human satisfaction. Multiple studies in the United States, Iceland, Spain, Belgium, and South Africa have shown that companies who have attempted a four-day workweek, for example, note an increase in employee satisfaction, reduced burnout and turnover, and no impact to productivity despite working fewer hours (notably, this coincides with a reduction in hours worked, but not a reduction in pay).[12] Similar results are shown in organizations who attempt a six-hour workday.[13] If working *less* means we can enjoy life more and still get the same work done, we must ask ourselves, why in the world are we working so much?

THE PARADOX OF TOIL

I have attempted at length so far to distance ourselves, as followers of Christ, from viewing our current way of work as the "normal" or "right" way to approach work. Like asking a fish to explain why water is wet, we have become so accustomed to the way things are now that the suggestion that they could be any different seems foreign to some, even threatening to others. I have heard more than a few well-meaning Christians cry, "Socialism!" at the mention of reductions in work time. I've even heard rants against the emergence of the work-from-home phenomenon from more than a couple of pulpits, bemoaning the laziness of entitled Millennials as the antithesis of the Bible's call to work diligently. (We Millennials are, after all, responsible for all of the trouble in the world!)

But we betray our ignorance when we associate calls for better work-life balances as the encroachment of socialism upon capitalism. After all, the status quo to which many American Christians cling—the eight-hour workday—was a social change whose origins in the mid-nineteenth century are, ironically, linked to the socioeconomic philosophies of Karl Marx.[14]

We also betray our lack of critical thinking when we don't take into account that, on the whole, our calendar-obsessed notions of laziness are dramatically different from those warned about in Scripture. Modern technology has given you and me the capability to be more "productive"—by emails sent, AI-generated presentations created in Canva, books listened to on Audible, outlines or strategies created in seconds by ChatGPT, and more—more than any figure in biblical history could have imagined being able to accomplish in a lifetime. We're in far greater danger of toiling, enslaved to the bondage of avarice and the clamoring noise of busyness to avoid introspection and contemplation—not to mention constant online connection at the expense of meaningful relationships.

Digital technology, and AI in particular, is a tremendous gift to us. It is yet another technological advancement that promises to gift back to us more time. It is the same unfulfilled promise made by previous technological advancements.

How we steward the gift of emerging technologies like AI will have enormous impact on the type of people we become. We can use AI to increase our productivity and generate more open space in our lives. But what we do with that open space is where I believe we need to pause, take inventory of our lives, and suggest a different way forward as a society—and I believe the church is an ideal institution to lead a better way forward, both for the individual and for the societies to which God calls the church. I want to suggest two roads diverged and the road less traveled that we should choose to take. (I recognize I'm taking serious liberties with Robert Frost's meaning in his famously misunderstood poem, "The Road Not Taken.")

One road AI can take us is the wide road—the well-worn road that we'll inevitably take without much thinking. AI will gift us with time, white space on our calendar. Our addiction to busyness, to money making, and to platform building will inevitably demand we fill this space with more stuff to do. If I am a pastor of a local church using AI to help with sermon series planning—something that I know from personal, pre-ChatGPT experience, can take hours, if not days, to plan—I can generate a broad but cohesive plan for a sermon series calendar through a back-and-forth with AI prompts in a matter of a few minutes. The question is, what do I do with that time I now have free that was once occupied by series planning? I might fill it up by deciding I'm going to create a podcast, I might start a leadership coaching side hustle, I might launch a new ministry at the church—I might do *more* with the time given. So, inevitably, I do. Where for only a brief moment, my calendar was more manageable, my time more flexible, my capacity greater to be more relational, I've found a way for toil to creep back in, and I'm overextended once again.

The other road, the road "less traveled," as it were, would be to find meaningful pursuits to use that time freed up by the help of AI. Rather than filling our calendars with additional toil, what if we were to spend the time AI gives back to us time with meaning and purpose? What if we spent more time in nature? In prayer? With our spouses and children? What if we pursued a creative passion like art or poetry? What if we became more involved in our church and our community? What if we spent more time cultivating friendships with our neighbors?

I remember as a youth reading *The Power of Prayer* by E. M. Bounds, in which Bounds describes the lifestyles of great people in prayer in the history of Protestantism. More than one was described as feeling as though the pressures and busyness of life would swallow their prayer time if they did not vigorously defend it (which generally involved getting up in the early hours before the hustle of the day began). As a teenager, I found these stories a bit amusing because the people whose lives were so "busy" were from hundreds of years ago—before the internet, before phones, high speed transport, etc. Their idea of *busy* was my idea of *boring*.

But now, as an adult, I realize that the human capacity to fill time with toil is as old as humanity itself. We have simply compounded our capacity to do more in less time with technological advances—our instinctual embrace of toil is an ancient vice resulting from the rebellion of Eden. The human paradox is that while we innovate to resist toil, knowing at a deep, Creator-creation level that it is not God's original intent for humanity, we also simultaneously embrace it—our rebellious hearts are drawn to the curse of toil. So we create ways to outsource toil—from the wheel to the AI assistant, only to return to taking more upon our backs.

FREE TIME, SLOTH, AND THE RESISTANCE OF TOIL

For those of us who swim in the waters of industrial constructs of time and work, what I'm suggesting—that we should use AI to toil *less*—seems anathema. Is Korpi asking us to be lazy? Hardly.

In Himanen's critique of the industrial work construct, he notes that the chief end or purpose of work in our current work ethic is *work* itself (and its most recent iterations, *money*).[15] We bear witness to this even in the language we use. Humans are "workers," "laborers," a "workforce." We quite literally have "human resource" departments who manage not only the resources given to the humans in the organizations but, more aptly, manage the humans *as* a resource of the company. When organizations (and even ministries) want something *from* their human capital or want them to sacrifice for the sake of the work, they will use familial language ("this organization is like a family!"), but when the work must disadvantage the worker or demand greater degrees of toil, the language changes ("this is a place of business" or "ultimately, this is a corporation"). Work itself is the chief idol to which we all bow in the industrial work construct. Our time serves it. Our attention serves it. Our family is subservient to it. But only if we allow it.

The flip side of this vision of work is not laziness or sloth. If "workers" were to be less characterized by their work-centeredness and more by their humanity, they're not in much danger of becoming the dystopian, slothful Eloi of H. G. Wells's *Time Machine* (lest we forget, Wells envisioned the working class evolving into the Morlocks and the aristocracy was destined to become the Eloi). Our culture is so collectively pressed firmly against the bosom of toil that laziness is not truly the imminent danger that many people fear. Instead, we as God's people have a responsibility to cast vision for what life can look like in a postindustrial world. This vision should necessarily include a recapture of playfulness, community-centeredness, and active forms of leisure.

By this, I mean that we should seek to "automate away the boring bits" of "stupid, repetitive work" enough so that people have capacity for the freedom of what Plato called *scholē*—that is, the self-guided organization of time and pursuit of one's passion for meaning-making and creative goodness in the world.[16] In

other words, the information age (and AI in particular) should give
you and me greater freedom to have agency and self-determination
over how we spend our time. Then we can spend our time doing
meaningful things, which many at the end of their lives regret not
doing enough of.

I'm not suggesting that our time should be freed of toil so that
it can be replaced by passively consuming the creative work of
others—such as bingeing the latest hit on Netflix. While, like the
feeling of abandoning one's diet to consume a giant piece of
cheesecake in the middle of the day, there's certainly room in our
lives for checking out and chilling on the couch, there's much
greater value in the active sorts of leisure that don't orient our
free time around passive consumption. I can attest from personal
experience that life is far richer by *learning to bake* a good
cheesecake than by simply *buying* one at the grocery store.

To expand on the cheesecake metaphor (assuming that you're
not hungry and distracted by now), the freedom from toil that AI
can give us—this "road less traveled," where we pursue the more
meaningful, innovative, collaborative, and enriching bits of life—
gives us space for building lives that are more self-determined,
relationally rich, and passion-built than what the industrial work
construct can give us. We need to stop being "breadwinners" and
start learning to bake bread.

THE CHURCH AND THE MISSIONAL
PURSUIT OF PASSION

Our modern work constructs of eight-hour days and forty-hour
weeks are verifiably ill-suited for the information economy.
Industrial constructs are even less suited for the ministry of the
local church and Christian ministries, though many in North
America operate according to the principles of the industrial
economy. Our toil comes in a never-ended connectedness to our
work, excused by a "commitment to the call of God" and "working

for the kingdom." It comes in an incessant demand for creative output in videos, podcasts, sermons, lectures, meetings, and more with rigid timelines that give little space for true creativity to flourish. For volunteers in the local church, this often comes in the form of ever-increasing calendar demands and attempting to fit our skills and passions into preconstructed boxes of involvement in the local church.

Since the advent of the modern workweek, pastors have found the demands of ministry at serious odds with this structure of work. Ministry work just isn't linear, though we try to make it this way. It necessarily requires that we retreat to the lonely places to get alone with God, though mobile technology has made us "on call" even at the dinner table with our family. It makes our observance of the sabbath negotiable, movable, and interruptible.

But we don't have to be this way. AI should not simply increase our productivity and pace as technological advances have done before. It should add value to life, in accordance with our created design. And it should improve our capacity to set aside toil to discern God's call to participate in his reconciliatory mission in the world. This requires, however, that we intentionally and unapologetically walk this road. It won't be given to us.

What if we went back to the drawing board, sourcing wisdom from our spiritual mothers and fathers who have gone before us? What if the Christian church completely blew up the industrial work construct—doing away with forty-hour workweeks, scrapping eight-hour workdays, and creating something completely innovative within our communities? Rather than being enslaved by the mechanical time of the modern era, what if we leaned on the ancient wisdom of those who have gone before us (as well as our sisters and brothers in much of Africa and Latin America) and treated time as more relational, more relative, and less mechanical?[17]

What if the people of God led the way in leveraging the power of AI to create space to be people on mission instead of tools for

more content production? To use a previous example, rather than
filling the calendar with more "stuff" after completing the sermon
series planning, what if we found ways to be more present in our
communities? What if we used AI to optimize our systems, assimilation funnels, and growth pipelines so that we, the people
God has called as agents of reconciliation in the world, were focused on building tables for people to sit, share a piece of their
lives, and find transformation and healing? What if we automated
the boring bits to focus on the more excellent things?

Among local churches (especially larger churches managing
large staffs with larger, corporate structures) and Christian ministries, we should also consider the possibilities AI presents to
give freedom and self-determination back to the people who
work on our staffs. I'm convinced that as AI presents opportunities in the information economy for people to pursue self-
determined passions, churches who do not innovate to encourage
the use of those passions will lose staff. This means allowing
(even encouraging) staff to be polyworkers, working for the
church while also lending their expertise and passions in other
directions as well.

Following the stay-at-home orders of the coronavirus pandemic, there has been much ado about corporations (and more
than a few ministries) bemoaning how "nobody wants to work"
because people prefer flexible, remote, and nontraditional approaches to employment. What these organizations have failed to
realize is that the power of the industrial work construct from
which they've built their influence is crumbling. The opportunities AI gives to the average person to innovate and build something on their own is already significant and rapidly growing. For
churches and ministries to be able to survive in the years to come,
we must innovate around the trend. To use the popular decla-
ration of the Borg from *Star Trek: The Next Generation*: "resistance is futile."

For Christian ministry, this will fundamentally require a shift in how we organize around mission. For much of the past several decades, North American evangelicalism has rallied around a "Moses model" to church vision. Moses (i.e., the senior pastor, church planter, ministry CEO, etc.) receives the organization's vision from the Lord, descends from the mountain top with that vision inscribed on tablets of stone (indicating their unflinchingly rigid nature), and disseminates that vision for the masses to follow without question or reservation. However, this model of church organization around mission has a rapidly approaching expiration date, due in part to the way in which that model has been used to abuse people and evade accountability (in both the corporate world as well as the church) and in part due to an increasing and important preference for forms of organizational life that are participatory and collaborative, and that invite feedback. This participatory form of organizational engagement is especially important for Millennials and Gen Zers, who are increasingly disengaged from church life—not because of atheism, but because of boredom.[18] It's not that these generations don't appreciate the value and role of the spiritual life—they just don't see the local church as having much to do with how they walk that out.

Christian ministries must necessarily innovate approaches to how we do mission together that form vision in a collective fashion—a model we see in the subtle foundation upon which the New Testament church was built. In this early church model, vision is not something God gives to an isolated apostolic superhuman, but to the community as a whole as they discern the leading of the Holy Spirit together, as they wrestle through community complexities and accountability together, and as they recognize the callings and giftings of the members of the group. Vision takes the shape of the people God brings, rather than people taking the shape of the vision given to them by a leader.

In an AI-driven information economy, we must begin to view churches and Christian ministries as communities that organize our visions primarily around God's redemptive mission in the world and, secondarily, around the particular and unique ways in which he has called the people within the church to carry that out. This requires that we view people less like automatons carrying out "the heart of the house" (as we've unfortunately been prone to doing, if we're honest). Instead, they are "networked creators," each with a call of God on their own life, and each entrusted to the church that they might be nurtured and equipped to participate in God's mission as they are uniquely designed to do. The mission, however, inherently belongs to the Lord—the callings he places upon people are unmediated by you and me as Christian leaders. Our task, therefore, is not to determine people's calling for them, but to discern alongside them and nurture it into maturity for the benefit of our communities and for the world.

The widespread integration of AI as an active tool in peoples' lives provides a tremendous opportunity for people to have resources at their disposal to pursue God's call on their lives while creating space for that passionate pursuit to be walked out. But the task of the church in this moment is to innovate and model a more excellent way out of our current approaches to work, which in our industrial-revolution hangover we simply cannot seem to shake.

We must model communities that renegotiate our relationship with time, recapturing its relational shape. We must model a joyful and enthusiastic pursuit of meaning-making, which Himanen calls the "hacker ethic" but which I see as a fundamentally Christian one, provided that the meaning-making we create in the world is oriented around God's design for humans to flourish and to be reconciled to Jesus.

Thus, for a Christian, an AI-influenced work life in a post-industrial economy is fundamentally concerned with the passionate pursuit of one's calling and giftings, creating goodness in our lives and in the lives of those around us to the glory of God. We can simply allow AI's presence in our lives to create space for more toil. But I'm convinced there's a road to take and—though it requires more intentionality, change, and discipline from us—it will yield far greater fruit in peoples' lives.

What would it mean for a local church to ethically and prayerfully integrate AI into its ministry practices, into its scheduling, design, and more—not to increase its capacity to do more, to toil more. What if instead, the local church stood out as a revolutionary reworking of what it means to use new technology to create space to improve human connection and increase the margin for reflection, prayer, and community engagement? What if the local church and not a maverick CEO showed a more excellent way to create healthy rhythms in its work, backing away from industrial-revolution forms of management and productivity and reimagining godly work in the age of AI? The church stands at an ideal place in human society to navigate a change out of the current commitment to toil and bondage to mechanical time and to model before the world the much-needed example of a people who can leverage the benefits of technology for the purpose of human flourishing.

9

PASTORAL CARE AND ARTIFICIAL CLERGY

DURING MY 2005 COLLEGE SUMMER BREAK, I did a pastoral internship at a predominantly Italian American Pentecostal church plant in the metropolitan Detroit area. It was my first up-close look at pastoral ministry at a church other than the one in which I came of age. The pastor was a great preacher but an even better shepherd, who sowed within me the transformational value of simply spending time with people (and, of course, usually over food, as Italians do so well). At that church I learned the value of receiving hospitality—nearly every evening I spent as a guest in someone else's home eating delicious food at their table, making memories together.

At that church I also learned how most pastors have impossible expectations placed on them. That same pastor who spent countless hours around tables with his congregation also told me many of his "what in the world?" stories—the sort of stories that almost all clergy have if they've served for very long. One such story was seared into my brain: one perfectly able-bodied parishioner who called him late at night at his home to ask him to pick up her prescription from Walgreens and then acted indignant when he declined.

Many subsequent stories have followed, both in my own experience in pastoral ministry as well as that of ministry friends. I've spoken with more than one music pastor who has simultaneously been rebuked for the music being both too loud and too quiet on the same Sunday. I've spoken with female clergy, one who was rebuked for wearing jeans on stage (because they might cause men to stumble) and another who was told how sexy she looked while wearing a cassock. Pastors often find themselves in no-win scenarios, either because of unrealistic expectations placed on them or because they are simply spread too thin.

While no-win scenarios do come with the territory, the ever-present demand to be all things to all people all the time can be mitigated to an extent by the integration of artificial intelligence (AI) into practices of pastoral care. In speaking with Christian leaders from around the world, I've found the intersection of AI and the pastorate to be where people are often the most reluctant to see the positive potential. And with good reason. Pastoral care relies on employing a great deal of wisdom that has been cultivated through the accumulation of experience over time. I'm confident AI will never be a replacement for wisdom. But AI does make for an excellent source for knowledge, and there are many ways in which it can be a complement to pastoral ministry that serves to better tend to the needs of their congregations while also lifting a bit of a load off the pastor's shoulders in the process. But this is not without its cautions.

The last several decades have produced increased expectations placed on clergy, exponentially greater than at any other time in history. In addition to being a shepherd and a preacher, pastors are also expected to be visionary leaders, strategists, CEOs, social media influencers, authors, conference headliners, coaches, and more. Increasingly, the strains of flattened wages and increased inflation make pastoring more difficult to be a sole focus. The modern pastor is expected to possess the skill set of a Fortune 500 executive with a median salary in the United States of about $55,000 a year—roughly what he or she would make selling cell phones at your nearest wireless retailer.[1] Is it any wonder, then, why pastors are burning out in record numbers and those who remain are categorized by life insurance companies in the same high-risk category as loggers and munitions workers?[2] The pressure to steer an organization into exponential growth and pick up all the prescriptions at Walgreen's can be exhausting.

Another dilemma faced by pastors at present is the reality of the clergy abuse crises that have been exposed en masse over the last number of years, in seemingly every corner of North American Christianity. Presently, scores of pastors reap the consequences of the sins of others being exposed. The pastor whose congregation is subsidizing his or her grocery bill must hear the public outcry that he or she has a housing allowance because a millionaire pastor he's never met can't help but cook the books. The pastor who desperately needs a ministry leader to mentor and develop her can't get her senior pastor to take a one-on-one meeting like he does other staff, because the high-profile pastor's sexual misdeeds in the town over reinforces her pastor's commitment not to meet alone with women. The pastor who is trying to give well-meaning spiritual life advice must give an account for the sins of the celebrity pastor whose church imploded over spiritual abuse.

Do not misunderstand my point. I am not in any way attempting to suggest that sin should be left unexposed. Hardly. I firmly believe that the exposure of such sin among the clergy is paramount to the purification and protection of Christ's bride. The blame for the ripple effect that ecclesial abuse has on the church rests squarely on the shoulders of the perpetrators, never the victims. So, to echo the words of Amos, "Let justice roll on like a river, righteousness like a never-failing stream!" (Amos 5:24). I only mean to highlight that part of the collateral damage of this present crisis is an increased burden on many overburdened but otherwise innocent pastors who are not engaged in nefarious sin. It is a heavy burden to bear to carry a call to help people but to be met with increased suspicion, often even hostility, as societal trust in the clergy continues to erode.

The modern ecclesial scandal crisis is a fruit of a broader set of issues in dire need of reform, in particular within American Protestantism. Sarah Billups groups this set of crisis-level issues into three categories: politics, culture, and the market. In other words, we're plagued by political idolatry, culture warring, and rampant consumerism.[3] (I would also add individualism.) This has produced a byproduct from which Billups named her book: "orphaned believers," those disaffected Christians who feel church-homeless yet dearly love Jesus. So, while the eroding trust in clergy often unfairly impacts trustworthy clergy, we must also consider how deeply it impacts those who are on the other end of the dilemma—those for whom trusting a pastor seems like a difficult task. Why does this matter? And what does it have to do with artificial intelligence? A lot, actually. Or at least, AI possesses incredible potential to aid in healing some of our present dilemmas. But it also may cause further harm.

MAKING ARTIFICIAL HEALERS

Dhruv Khullar's 2023 piece in the *New Yorker* titled "Talking to Ourselves: Can Artificial Minds Heal Real Ones?" reported on the rise of using AI in the field of mental health.[4] While using artificial simulations for therapy is not new (Khullar gives the example of a program called Eliza, created by Joseph Weizenbaum in the 1960s, designed to simulate Rogerian Therapy), the increased sophistication and adoption of AI has made its use more popular.

In 2017, for instance, Alison Darcy created a smartphone app called Woebot to simulate the practice of Cognitive Behavioral Therapy (CBT), one of the more widely used forms of therapy employed by mental health professionals. Other apps like Youper and Wysa also launched with similar aims. On Woebot and Darcy, Khullar notes,

> When Darcy was in graduate school, she treated dozens of hospitalized patients using C.B.T.; many experienced striking improvements but relapsed after they left the hospital. C.B.T. is "best done in small quantities over and over and over again," she told me. In the analog world, that sort of consistent, ongoing care is hard to find. . . . "No therapist can be there with you all day, every day," Darcy said. Although the company employs only about a hundred people, it has counselled nearly a million and a half, the majority of whom live in areas with a shortage of mental health providers.[5]

Upon reading this, I first thought, *There's no way people would get on board with reaching out to an AI bot for counseling.* But I couldn't have been more mistaken. In a time in which, Khullar notes, one in five Americans struggle with some form of mental illness—and also at a time where there is a tremendous labor shortage of mental health professionals to meet the need of the hour, AI mental health resources have become enormously popular.

If you've sought out the services of a mental health professional in recent years, there's a decent chance the wait time to get in to see a counselor or psychologist is long. For Americans, health insurance coverage issues often create obstacles. And when one does find a counselor, the counselor does what I have done myself as a pastor and college professor—provide one's phone number and invite a call or text at any time there's a felt need, but also set expectations that responses will come during business hours on the following day.

This is an understandable, even wise, practice. It provides a semblance of instantaneous availability but retains professional boundaries. It gives a sort of "illusion" (I mean that in the most well-meaning way) of immediacy yet allows the professional to tend to their own well-being and their own life.

This is laudable because counselors, like pastors (both of whom, along with physicians, Henri Nouwen groups in to the "healing professions"), are human beings.[6] They have limitations, incur vicarious and secondary trauma from those who they seek to help, and must tend to their own inner life as well as their outer relational spheres. In light of the ever-blurring lines between work life and home life, a plethora of studies have shown the psychological danger of always needing to be "on."

In times of significant personal crisis, the (understandable) unavailability of a mental health professional can be extremely difficult for persons seeking help. Those, like me, who have suffered under the weight of long-term anxiety, find that many of our most significant moments of internal wrestling come in the middle of the night. It comes not on a prescheduled time, but in the fading hours of a Sunday night before the beginning of the next workweek. And these are generally the moments when a qualified person is unavailable to assist.

Often these are not moments of critical crisis, but of, as Woebot described to one user who leaned on its services between counseling visits, moments of ruminating and catastrophic thinking.[7] In these moments, users are not duped into thinking they're speaking to a human. They know full and well that they're talking to an algorithm. They just don't care. The algorithm walks them through basic mental health triaging, and they find comfort in it. Like Replika, Woebot and other mental health chatbots fill the white space between relationships where necessary professional boundaries and limitations of human presence exist. They do not replace the need for mental health professionals (nor are they likely to ever do so) but instead act as a first line of defense in the efforts to improve people's mental health, potentially opening time and space for human professionals to navigate more complex and serious cases.

A VISION FOR PASTORAL AI

Like the growing trend of AI devoted to mental health, there is an equally urgent need for vision in developing "pastoral AI." I recognize that this may sound startling to some, but let me clarify what I mean. I'm not suggesting that AI bots can actually be pastors, which is no more reasonable than to call Woebot a psychologist. But as with the mental health profession, there is a need for an artificial aid to function in a triaging and frontline capacity, not to replace the work of the pastor, but to complement it in certain areas, and to supplement it in times when the pastor cannot (or need not) be present. Allow me to articulate several reasons why I believe such a resource is necessary and what potential shapes pastoral AI could take.

First, pastoral AI can provide some lift to the load carried by an increasingly overworked and underpaid pastoral labor force. It can serve as the faceless yet gentle responder who lets a dear congregant know that her pastor is not available to DoorDash her Walgreens order for her. Where such human-to-human conversations almost always are the source of conflict (or at least the genesis of a night's worth of anxiety in the mind of a pastor, over whether such a conflict might arise), a pastoral AI can deal with the triaging conversations. A pastoral AI, embedded on the church's website or a smartphone app could potentially serve to navigate some of the more basic demands on pastors—like "What does 'baptized for the dead' mean in 1 Corinthians 15:29?" It can assist congregants wanting to get involved in a small group or discipleship class. It can guide people along in discipleship resourcing as well as potentially engage in some of the information-dissemination facets of a person's discipleship journey.

The danger here is that evangelicals, especially in the West, already overassociate discipleship with information retention. So the temptation of a resource that could facilitate much of the dissemination of information to individuals—especially when it can customize that information based on an algorithmic insight—is to remove the human component to congregational formation, especially in churches that depend heavily on growth models that already tend to overly systematize the process of "pipelining" people through a spiritual journey. Having led on the pastoral staff of a megachurch myself, I am deeply aware of the challenges of attempting to disciple large numbers of people at the same time, especially when there is an underlying culture of productivity that prioritizes speedy solutions. In such environments, such an AI tool could be enormously problematic, further removing the human-centric characteristic of discipleship in the name of streamlining processes and maximizing effectiveness. To reinforce the point I made earlier, AI cannot replace either the wisdom of human experience or the discernment we enjoy from the Holy Spirit. This is where we find the limitations of machines and a unique dynamic of what it means to bear God's image to the world. AI in this capacity should be strictly regarded as a complement, not a supplement.

I remain firmly convinced of two things on this matter: Pastoral AI has profound potential to alleviate the burden of the more basic functions of a pastor's week. And such a tool must function as a triaging agent, complementing and ultimately pointing to the formation that takes place in human-to-human communication. We simply cannot resource people with information and expect them to become well-formed, fully devoted followers of Jesus. Ours is an incarnational faith, as modeled to us by the God who became man and tabernacled among us.

Second, I am cautiously optimistic about the potential of a pastoral AI to assist in basic pastoral counseling responsibilities. This, of course, depends largely on what information such AI algorithms are given to learn. AI that feeds on data provided (with permission and compensation) by pastoral exemplars would yield a much different sort of pastoral counselor than that of the bottom shelf "three steps to a better you (and Jesus in there somewhere, too)" variety of self-help resources. But a properly formed AI bot could potentially aid in the basic counsel a pastor might provide, especially in off-hour times when a human pastor is unavailable.

One facet that I find particularly helpful is that such a bot could be paired with CBT and other professional mental health therapy techniques, yielding a bot that not only could function both in providing pastoral insight, but also basic mental health services. What's more, such a tool could serve to recommend users to appropriate parties when a handoff is necessary, either to a pastor or to a licensed mental health professional, depending on the needs of the moment. Ideally, this could serve to mitigate instances of people getting improper mental health advice from well-meaning but unqualified pastors.

Another area I envision AI serving pastoral counseling needs is the potential of machine learning to inform premarital counseling—a practice that routinely relies on data gathering through assessments. Some external insight can be provided to pastors when such assessments are taken, though much of the interpretation of the data still relies on the experiential knowledge of the pastor. Machine learning–powered assessments or other forms of data collection for engaged couples could provide much richer interpretations and recommendations—giving a pastor who is conducting premarital counseling a sort of "counseling assistant," secondary to the discerning work of the pastorate, pointing people to resources, providing a semblance of empathy—though it would ultimately be limited in its capacity to exercise God-given wisdom. Humans cultivate this wisdom not through the curation of large language models of data acquisition, but through pain and hardship, trial and error, and from the Spirit of God teaching us along the way.

I conducted an experiment of my own (albeit, very brief and very unscientific) using ChatGPT-4. I prompted ChatGPT to "help me walk my own family situation through Murray Bowen's Family Systems Theory." ChatGPT outlined Bowen's eight interlocking concepts of family systems theory (FST) and provided two bullet-point insights for consideration under each concept. It then invited me to explore the concepts more thoroughly. I responded with "Please walk me through each of these in a series of question-and-answer prompts. Gather all my responses and, after we've finished walking through all of the concepts, create a summary that describes how Murray Bowen would have diagnosed my family."

Within seconds, ChatGPT developed an assessment for me to take using Bowen's FST framework. Once I answered all the questions, it analyzed the data and offered a breakdown of concept-by-concept insights into my family dynamic. I then asked it to offer a summary analysis with recommendations for improving areas of growth as though it were Murray Bowen. ChatGPT provided a series of such recommendations that were quite profound and insightful given how little time the entire process took.

A more intentional form of such an analysis that not only incorporates one conceptual framework like Bowen's FST, but others as well, could provide invaluable insight to pastors seeking to prepare couples for marriage or to help couples who are already married. And this could be further enhanced by other forms of data collection that can give insights into a person's behavioral psychology. Too often such data has been collected by machine learning for the purposes of engaging the human as a consumer or for political purposes. But I believe we've yet to unlock the full potential of responsibly sourced data for the purposes of life enrichment, spiritual formation, and community enhancement.

Third, pastoral AI represents an opportunity to aid in pastoral care because people may be less inclined to be inauthentic in online communication in general, and in chatbot communication more specifically. During our initial phase of research in 2023, while leading the research for the Digital Mission Consortia, one of the insights we noted was that while church leaders often assume people are less authentic online, even misrepresenting themselves, this is largely a myth. People are no more inclined to misrepresent themselves online than they are in physical situations.[8]

If we take a moment to pause and reflect about all the jokes we make about how church people represent themselves on Sunday morning (our family itself has had more than one argumentative car ride to church only to walk in with big smiles on our faces), we can see how the assumption that people are more likely to misrepresent themselves online than in physical ministry settings is a bit silly. The data refutes it, and our own perception of having our "church faces" on reminds us that people are very much inclined to misrepresent themselves in physical ministry settings as well. One could argue that the possibility for misrepresentation is greater in person than online, where anonymity provides a cover to be authentic in a way that face-to-face forms of mediated communication cannot.

This matters especially when we consider how to best minister to digitally native generations like Gen Z and Generation Alpha, whose relational constructs depend more heavily on internet communication than those of us who grew up in times where we can recall not having the internet. It also matters for those who have been victim to spiritual abuse and church trauma, where a pastoral AI resource can be a bridge in a time when a person is too reluctant to speak to a human pastor.

When we couple our understanding that people are more inclined to be open and authentic online with insights from anthropomorphized forms of AI like Replika and Woebot, then it is reasonable to foresee how a pastorally minded AI, fed with knowledge of Christianity's best pastoral theologians (think Eugene Peterson and Dallas Willard), could be an enormously helpful tool in complementing human pastoral care in the years to come.

Will AI replace the vocation of pastor? Hardly. Will it disrupt it and change it? Absolutely. Like in many professions, the way that pastors shepherd their churches will be undoubtedly changed by AI tools to aid in that shepherding task and in the emerging need for AI stewardship to be a discipleship issue.

Where pastors perhaps position themselves best in the emerging present is to shift from viewing one's vocation as a "sage on the stage" (a divinely called dispenser of religious knowledge) and instead a "guide on the side" (one entrusted with tending to and safeguarding the health and vitality of Christian communities). In a piece I wrote in 2023, I said that pastors will need to be increasingly more cognizant of the environments they are creating and how those environments contribute to the flourishing of their congregation and the broader community:

> This attentiveness to environments has less to do with creating a high production worship experience on Sundays, and more to do with a broader ecosystem of environments where people can encounter the living God together, shaping their formation in a holistic way. Flourishing community environments are deeply concerned not just with scriptural truth, but also people's ability to deepen relationships with one another, engage in justice and mercy work, and is safeguarded against the corruption and abuse that has become all too common in ecclesial spaces. Flourishing communities steward people as image bearers, not simply as consumers of content and information.[9]

Thus, the role of the pastor must necessarily shift to something much more ancient, before our modern pedagogical practices took central priority. The pastor of the future will necessarily look less like a modern version of a Greek philosopher, providing wisdom to the masses, and instead more like the biblical image of a gardener—entrusted with the care and nurturing of the plant and the conditions that give the plant opportunity for growth. As pastors step into their role of tending to sacred and flourishing

Christian community, they step into a space where AI simply cannot be a substitute.

But AI can be a tool, like a spade or a pair of shears in the hand of the gardener. But tending to the harvest requires the sacred relationship between human and divine. We tend to the conditions that encourages one to grow and bear fruit while God himself bears the fruit in people's lives. That's a spiritual vocation that simply cannot be replaced with AI. But AI can certainly be a valuable tool in the gardener's hands.

10

AI AND CHRISTIAN HIGHER EDUCATION

In 2005 I arrived on the campus of Central Bible College (CBC) in Springfield, Missouri. At the time, CBC was the flagship institution of the Assemblies of God in the United States, "for the training of ministers and missionaries" (its longtime motto). At one time, CBC's library allegedly had one of the largest collections of Pentecostal resources on the planet, and despite being a relatively small school, CBC provided one of the best undergraduate ministry educations I have ever encountered. (It has since merged with its sister liberal arts institution, Evangel University.) I often joke with my undergraduate students how I feel like a relic, having attended school at a time when I still had to print off my papers and hand them in to the professor. I never encountered an online learning management system (LMS) until after my time at CBC.

Another aspect of my undergraduate years that makes me often feel like a relic is recalling the parameters of the syllabi for most of the classes I took during my time there. In addition to specific style, length, font, and spacing requirements were resource requirements. While that's still common today—professors requiring certain parameters around the number and type of sources used—what seems archaic is the *location* from which references could be sourced. If a paper required five to seven sources, only two or three were generally permitted to be sourced from the internet. The rest had to come from physical books, often making the campus library a zoo during midterms and finals.

This requirement wasn't an aberration or a bug—it was a mainstay. It was so common I assume it was likely a requirement of the school rather than the preference of the faculty. At the time, the requirement didn't seem odd. After all, we had a phenomenal library. Why wouldn't the school want us to use it?

But fast forward only a few years, and such a staunch regulation is nothing more than the outdated preference of a bygone era. Most schools, including the institutions at which I teach, provide enormous portions of their library online for immediate access. When I was a student at Fuller, I practically lived in the online library and its network of ebooks, academic databases, and interlibrary loan request service. My undergraduate students at Ascent College, where I serve as Dean of Digital Ministries, have a vast majority of their required texts available online. While I did my undergraduate work in a time when online resources were severely restricted, I'm not sure that at any of the schools where I teach, I could even *submit* a syllabus that prohibited online resource access and see it approved.

Times change.

I'm convinced we are at a similar moment with artificial intelligence and higher education, not only within Christian higher education, but as a whole. Almost as soon as generative artificial intelligence (AI) models began to be widely used, there emerged a spectrum of postures within academia, ranging from reluctant to outright hostile. While some schools were more proactive than others to issue AI-use policies, 2023 was something of the Wild West for professors trying to navigate how to think about AI, prevent AI plagiarism, and more.

Since that time, schools have landed on a variety of positions and policies concerning AI and have adopted tools to attempt to catch the use of generative AI for the creation of written content. Long-standing tools like Turnitin integrated AI detection tools into their platforms, but schools have found these detection tools to have a mixed bag of results. For example, ZeroGPT (an AI plagiarism detection software) returned a 94% certainty rating that the United States Constitution was written by artificial intelligence. Originality.ai had a 60% certainty score for the same test.[1] Turnitin's own website points out that it is not always accurate and should not be used as the sole basis for adverse action against a student.[2] But the three-way battle between students, institutions of higher learning, and generative AI wages on, often with professors woefully ill equipped to navigate the battlefield.

A CASE STUDY IN MISTAKEN AI-DENTITY

I spoke with a master's student at an evangelical seminary in the United States who told me a startling story of AI detection gone awry. The seminary had a basic AI-use policy that essentially prohibited students from using AI for content creation, but allowed it as an aid in research, editing, and ideation. Following the policy's allowance for AI in the editing process, the student regularly employed the help of Grammarly, after writing an initial rough draft, to polish the language (as any good editing tool does). Grammarly would then provide a downloadable file of a new, fair draft copy of the paper, which the student would check one final time and then turn in.

As the course was coming to a close, the student received an email from the professor, indicating that Turnitin's AI detection tool returned a series of high percentile scores on several of the student's papers. The professor informed the student that this constituted cheating and that the student would receive a zero score on each of the assignments that Turnitin had flagged. If the student wished to discuss it further, the professor directed the student to take the matter up with the dean who, along with the president of the seminary, had been copied in the email.

The student was initially humiliated, enraged, and felt shame that such an accusation had come without any further dialogue. "You're a cheater!" was the conclusion, and there was to be no further discussion on the matter. However, the student pushed back to both the dean and the professor, offering to submit the initial rough drafts as evidence, provide photos of the physical books used in the research process, and even take an oral exam to prove competency on the relevant subject matters. The student cited Turnitin's own caution about how its tool is to be used in disciplinary proceedings, as well as case study examples of other schools who have abandoned the use of AI detection software altogether. After a bit of back-and-forth, the professor eventually relented and returned the student's grades, but not without a cautionary warning that the school would be updating its policy to further restrict the use of AI in the editing process.

This seminary student's experience was just one example of the uninformed, inconsistent, and often hostile frontier that is the intersection of academia and the proliferated use of AI in academic writing. While this student's issue was resolved fairly quickly, due undoubtedly to a reasonable dean and a professor who was willing to admit a mistake, some students who encounter these sorts of issues must endure much more. And professors and institutions alike are often ill equipped to navigate the terrain with any measure of certainty.

But, similar to the changes that befell academia after my time as an undergraduate student searching my campus library for the required number of physical books, so too we're at the beginning of another set of dramatic changes in the relationship between technology and learning that is going to dramatically change the way we do higher education.

Christian institutions don't have a particular leg up in the conversation or a unique solution to the AI and learning dilemma. However, I'm convinced that our capacity to lead the way in innovation while upholding sound integrity is a contribution we can make to society to the glory of God. I want to turn now to address several key issues within the ongoing conversation of AI and education. I will give a disclaimer that some of my ideas are a little spicy—suggestions that while odd or unusual in the landscape of the current conversation, I'm convinced are necessary to move the conversation in the direction it needs to go—and ultimately *will* go, whether we like it or not. Like many of the other subjects addressed in this book, these suggestions are meant to invite further dialogue as we work out what it means to be the people of God in the age of AI. This isn't the conclusion of the conversation (i.e., a mic drop moment as it were), but rather an invitation to continue a conversation that requires all our participation.

THE ETHICS OF AI: A PREDICTION OF THE FUTURE

The basis for much of my argument is founded in assumptions not about pedagogy, but about ethics. Ethics are, by nature, a set of principles born from a culture's deepest level of a shared worldview. Our ethics, therefore, evolve over time through collective dialogue. No one person can bring about a change in a society's ethics through universal decree or threat of force (though a singular person can dramatically impact a culture's ethics, as we've seen in the rise of bombastic populist figures in global politics). Our ethics are collectively determined and are continuously evolving.

We see this in the example of my time at CBC. What was a best practice born from a sense of rightness has evolved to now be something of yesteryear. We are now in a time of renegotiating our ethics around what it means to "write," the correct process of ideation and creation with integrity, and to some extent even the concept of plagiarism itself, which is a chief concern for academic institutions as it concerns student (and professorial) use of AI.

While I'm neither a time-traveler nor a fortuneteller, I am convinced that the ongoing proliferation of AI use in everyday life, work, passion projects, and education is going to dramatically alter the human relationship with the idea of what it means to create. In the not-so-distant future, I believe AI will inevitably be an *expected* (not simply permissible) part of what it means for a creator to generate any number of artifacts, whether visual, auditory, or written, similar to how the use of spellcheck and grammar check are assumed tools in the writing process today. The idea of regulating the use of AI, or the time spent in detecting its use (to which we are devoting so much effort at present) will be perceived as a wasteful expenditure of time from the dusty old 2020s when people were still afraid of AI.

Instead, as it pertains specifically to education, I predict that students' work will be judged, in part, by their capacity to use AI well in the process of creating written work. Time and attention given to the right structure and format of a paper, citation errors, and even the formation and argumentation of a thesis will be considered basic nonnegotiables, comparable to putting one's name on a paper or not writing an academic paper in Comic Sans font. AI already makes much of this incredibly easy to do. Instead, the richness and depth of reflection will be a key focus for grading—as generative AI struggles to write well much beyond the depth of the simple organization and summarization of knowledge.

I also believe that alternative forms of testing knowledge will be more commonplace, such as oral exams and the creation of artifacts that we now consider more avant-garde forms of assignments (creating a podcast, an e-course, etc.). For Christian institutions, this should necessarily take a turn toward students creating from the knowledge learned, given both that teaching others is a desired outcome in the preparation of students for ministry and that the capacity to create from knowledge represents the pinnacle of learning.[3]

Much of the effort currently devoted to detecting AI, and even citing the use of AI, will ultimately be futile. Fifty years from now, I suspect professors will regard the practice of citing the use of AI in an academic paper in much the same way I might respond to a student who cited the use of her computer's Word Processor today. It's wholly unnecessary because it's an assumed, normal practice.

Many of the popular LMS platforms used in higher education today are behind the times in understanding how students learn, how technology interfaces with the creation of courses, and how students interact with courses. But I suspect that someday (perhaps, many years from now), AI will also be a mainstay resource in the process of creating an academic course, even facilitating the learning process in the course itself.

AI has the capacity (and I believe the learning experience would be enriched because of it) to conduct learning needs assessments (i.e., a pretest) at the beginning of a class and custom-build a suite of lectures, resources, and even assignments to create hand-tailored learning programs for each student, pursuant to the learning outcomes of a course, adjusting the learning experience to meet accessibility, cultural, and linguistic needs along the way (e.g., auditory-oriented assignments for certain learners and real-time translation of material for students enrolled at a school where the primary language is one other than their own). Using benchmark data capture practices as a student learns, AI will be able to make corrections to the learning journey to ensure outcomes are met. Cohort learning will focus more on the synthesis and sharing of learning experiences and their intersection with personal experience, a dialogue-based approach to learning called "andragogy" that is currently employed in many adult learning environments (and popularized through thinkers like Jane Vella and Malcolm Knowles)—but not without similar group-oriented approaches to learning in younger people (such as play-based learning and Montessori models of education). But what then will the role of the professor be in this AI-driven picture of higher education in the future?

SAGE ON THE STAGE VERSUS GUIDE ON THE SIDE

In the West, the primary method of education has generally defaulted to a monodirectional pedagogy. This is true in the academy and in the church alike. If we want people to learn, we must gather them together so that the person who has already learned may impart the knowledge through a lecture. The deposit of that knowledge in the learner is subsequently checked through a variety of quality control methods (tests, quizzes, papers, etc.). The educator then, like the pastor, has primarily functioned as a dispenser of knowledge—a mighty sage on the stage to gaze upon with reverence and adoration. Throngs of learners might gather around that sage to gather knowledge, like peasants seeking loaves of bread distributed in a medieval town square at the command of the nobility.

This description is undoubtedly hyperbolic. The effectiveness of this sage-on-the-stage method has been challenged over the years for many reasons. But as AI (and digital technology in general) has become more widely used in higher education, the *effectiveness* of the sage-on-the-stage approach to education isn't the primary issue so much as the *viability* of the approach. When AI can dispense more knowledge in a moment than any one professor could ever hope to accumulate and dispense in a month, is there a need for a professor? Can't we all simply be self-guided on our quest for whatever preferred STEM degree we choose so that our society might churn out "wage earners," "laborers," and "entrepreneurs" and thereby feed the neoliberal market-driven economy and fuel our unquenchable avarice as a society? What possible need could there be for a sage on the stage when digital platforms have replaced the lecture hall stage and artificial intelligence is the Plato of all sages?

Undoubtedly there is some significant tendency toward a sort of individualized, self-driven, even à la carte approach to learning, which we already see in nonaccredited online learning programs. But there is still a place for the professor, both in the tumult of the present moment and in an AI-powered learning system of the future that many today may worry is dystopian. I, on the other hand, view AI-driven learning as an opportunity to recover a more effective space for the educator, one that is ancient, holy even—that is, in educators shifting from viewing themselves as sages on the stage to guides on the side.

These catchy sorts of terms have been around for a while. The idea is, as I argued for the shift in the role of pastor previously, that educators must view themselves as a colaborer in the learning process, providing wisdom, assisting with application, guiding to deeper evaluation, and providing a greater focus on helping learners become *who* they need to be while the knowledge acquisition process helps them learn *what* they need to learn. A guide on the side cannot be the relationally distant "ivory tower" educator that many people think of when they think of college education (though this has largely gone the way of the dodo, especially in Christian education). Instead, they are like the Sherpa people of Tibet and Nepal, many of whom assist climbers in the summiting of mountains. Sherpas are not simply concerned with passing on technique (e.g., "put your foot there," "follow this path") but instead also embody a hardiness, resilience, and expertise that serves as a model for climbers to learn from and emulate.

A guide on the side in an AI-driven educational process should be no different. While AI can source, categorize, customize, recommend, and individualize the learning process, Christian educators of the future will necessarily require a posture that seeks to assist in the application of knowledge, to cultivate wisdom, and to share in the development of internal character qualities—spiritual formation that AI is simply ill equipped to do. This vision for a guide on the side in an AI-driven educational future necessarily requires at least four significant shifts in the way educators think about learning today.

Shift one: From information impartation to wisdom impartation. Educators must become savvier and more discerning about helping learners know how to steward knowledge well, not simply determining whether they possess knowledge. We live in a seemingly paradoxical time in human history where the masses simultaneously possess the greatest degree of access to the whole canon of human knowledge in their pocket *while* simultaneously existing without any degree of discernible wisdom in knowing how to live well as human beings in society.

The place of the educator must necessarily include the cultivation of wisdom in the learning process instead of disseminating and checking for the retention of information alone. I've witnessed this in my relationships with many professors and have attempted to embody this practice myself in teaching in colleges and seminaries. My primary objective is that students learn how to pastorally apply knowledge, not simply retain it. The place where educators must thrive in the future is, ironically enough, in cultivating the skill set that makes us reflect most fondly on educators who have made the biggest impact in our lives—those who took a personal interest in us, imparted something intangible but vital in our lives, helped us apply the knowledge we learned, and embodied something we hoped to become.

Shift two: From competency formation to virtue formation. While AI will likely hand tailor and automate the process of competency development and assessment of competency, it cannot account for the internal qualities that make good people good. Educators of the future must consider their role in the formation of virtues and the mitigation of vices in the lives of those to whom they're entrusted. In this regard, there is a rabbinic shape to these sorts of guides on the side, like Jesus himself, who spent precious little time explicitly teaching doctrine and much more time teaching the ethics of the kingdom (and the application thereof).

The Sermon on the Mount is so powerfully radicalizing not because it was a soporific expository lecture, but precisely because it was *not* that. Instead, Jesus painted a picture of the upside-down ethics of the kingdom in such a way that it was universally applicable to the lives of every one of his followers, regardless of the particulars of their individual vocations. It remains radically applicable to us today. In Rabbi Jesus, we have the ideal vision of the flourishing educator in the age of AI: one who is deeply concerned, yet also indescribably patient, with helping his followers become who they need to be while they do what they are meant to do.

We live in a time when even Christians seem to readily dispense with a need for sound character in a leader, provided that they produce the right results. We say, "Yeah, but he gets the job done!" when justifying the moral bankruptcy of a political leader and, "Yeah, but look at the fruit their ministry produces!" when justifying the moral bankruptcy of a spiritual leader. I believe part of the way we recover this is a deeper concern and focus within Christian education in the future that forms learners of all stages to lead from the overflow of a well-formed inner life. Dallas Willard says this,

> We must clearly understand that there is rigorous consistency in the human self and its actions. This is only of the things we are most inclined to deceive ourselves about. If I do evil, I am the kind of person who does evil; if I do good, I am the kind of person who does good (1 John 3:7-10). Actions are not

impositions on who we are, but are expressions of who we are. They come out of our heart and the inner realities it supervises and interacts with.[4]

It would seem that in God's economy there is no category for "pastor who abuses his staff but is a man of God because his ministry is growing" or "Christian businesswoman who cheats on her husband but who is a woman of God because of her Bible knowledge," as we have become all too comfortable with. Instead, *who* we are becoming in the process of our growth—that internal cultivation of virtues and constraint of vices—matter immensely to God. And there are few, outside of parents and local church pastors, who possess the power to radically influence the formation of virtue in people more than the educators they encounter as they develop.

There has been much conversation over the last several years, as the future of many Christian academic institutions is uncertain, about the need to recover the ancient role the "pastor-theologian" once played in the life of the church. Most of the leaders of ancient Christianity, like Polycarp of Smyrna, possessed a combination of tremendous theological brilliance and pastoral leadership over local churches. The pastors *were* the theologians; the theologians *were* the pastors. As the concept of a monovocational professor and a monovocational pastor both become increasingly difficult vocations to sustain—and as Christian academic institutions increasingly adopt franchise models whereby extension sites are run through local churches—the two worlds of academy and local church will overlap more and more.

A key distinction in this shift must be toward the emergence of not simply a pastor-theologian (that is, a theologically trained and gifted person who also holds a pastoral office), but in the recovery of the *pastoral* theologian—the sort of theologian who is trained and gifted in stewarding the well-being and formation of those entrusted to themselves, regardless of whether they are in a classroom or in a sanctuary. For the pastoral theologian, theology and church leadership alike are an incarnational enterprise, forming people with the virtue and character necessary to sustain them in life and give the church integrity in her witness.

Many professors in Christian education with whom I am acquainted already have a pastoral bent to them. Many have also served as pastors or missionaries at some point in their lives, bringing a heart to shepherd students, not simply disseminate disembodied doctrines for student assimilation. In an education landscape that will increasingly be dominated by AI, I believe these sorts of educators will thrive most. Those who hold onto traditional notions of pedagogy that are concerned solely with the flat absorption and retention of information (or, worse yet, the fulfillment of teaching obligations imposed by the school as a way to pursue their true passions of research and writing), will likely struggle to find footing in the emerging normal.

Shift three: From monologue-based learning to dialogue-based learning. Learning in an AI-driven world will increasingly become more dialogical and participatory. Vella and Knowles's andragogy has been a learning concept applied specifically to adults because it depends on an existing framework of knowledge and experience upon which the learning environment can be built. Rather than a monodirectional form of learning, from sage to student, andragogy creates a multidirectional learning environment wherein learning takes place from facilitator to student, between students, and even from students to facilitator.

In a world where knowledge is easily accessible and where AI accelerates and curates that accessibility, andragogical forms of learning can easily be adapted to younger learners. I have found that in learning environments with tech-equipped teenagers and twentysomethings, if I give them space to speak, their preexisting questions and assumptions (often informed by internet inquiries they've already done) can guide the learning environment. My role in those moments shifts toward stewarding the dialogue, keeping it on track, offering wisdom, provoking respectful debate, and more.

I experienced one such learning environment not long ago when I was invited to speak with a group of students in the Potomac School of Leadership. I came prepared with an outline of items *I* wanted to cover. But at the beginning of our ninety minutes together, I opened the floor to them to ask the questions they were wrestling with, on the subject we were discussing. The conversation continued for almost the entire duration of our time together and, it just so happened, I was able to cover most of what was on my outline through the discussion rather than needing to interrupt it.

AI-driven learning will require educators to develop the skills of dialogue stewardship, helping students learn in small groups and teams, and guiding the learning process through a clear sequence that takes learners on a journey toward more advanced concepts.[5] While teenagers and twentysomethings do not possess the life experience of adult learners, they are capable of sourcing information with incredible speed and savvy. They often come to learning environments already preloaded with knowledge and opinion. Facilitators need to know, therefore, how to help young learners sort through it, apply wisdom to it, be equipped to apply the learning to their life and context, and build trusted relationships with those alongside them in the learning process.

Shift four: From high control to low control. One of the most significant challenges I've observed among Christian leaders when attempting to adapt to our digital world, be it in the academy or in the local church, is in the release of control. The digital age has forever democratized and decentralized the acquisition and dissemination of knowledge. To an extent, I'm convinced that this struggle is born from a conscious-level desire for people to embrace what we perceive to be orthodox doctrines and live morally upright lives. But at an unconscious level, this struggle is born from issues concerning our own fear and desire for power. And if we are to take an honest assessment of how high levels of control over knowledge and behavior have impacted the church throughout history, it is not a pretty picture.

AI empowers learners not only to retain knowledge, but to turn around and do something with it, often inviting a process of communal theologizing through sharing reflections and insights on social media. Today's learners are not simply "learners." Rather, they are "networked creators," each possessing the ability to create based on what they've learned and disseminate it throughout social networks on various platforms. In this regard, the old broadcast form of "one to many" communication is dead. Instead, learners communicate in a "many to many" form, sharing ideas that inevitably invite dialogue in the comment sections of social media platforms.[6]

Properly empowering this new normal necessitates abandoning notions of control and instead focusing on formation. In my backyard garden, I grow, among other things, tomatoes (inevitably a greater sum than I need, too). I have absolutely no control over how each of my tomato plants naturally grows. I have no ability to control that a new branch starts here and not there or that the plant bears fruit on this branch and not that one. What I *can* do is provide structure that encourages natural growth in a particular way. I can trellis, tie, prune, stake, and more so that the environment in which the tomato plant matures encourages a particular growth outcome. But if I cage too much, prune too much, or bend a branch too much to tie it off, I'll inevitably do great harm—perhaps even kill—the plant I want so badly to bear good fruit.

The same is true in low control forms of learning. We must cultivate environments that encourage growth in a particular direction (accompanied by the previously mentioned emphasis on wisdom and virtue formation) without restraining it in a way that harms. We need to consider how to empower students with the ability to live as networked creators in the digital age, not simply as passive recipients of knowledge.

USING AI WELL TODAY

AI will radically change the landscape of learning in the future, but we also must wrestle through this inflection-point moment we're in at present. The recent emergence of AI into the public conversation has generated a cacophony of opinions on how AI should be used in education (specifically by students). This conversational chaos is an inevitable requirement as humans, in our various expressions of community, renegotiate our ethics in light of challenges to them—challenges like artificial intelligence.

While the impact of AI on the actual construction and execution of a course will almost certainly be the biggest impact of AI on higher education, what is getting most of the attention in the current conversation is concerns about student plagiarism. Schools have issued a variety of policies on the use of generative AI (like ChatGPT) in recent years, most of which will serve as temporary stabilizing points as the cultural conversation continues. But I suspect most of the AI-use policies issued now will look dramatically different in the future, if they even exist at all. This is due, in part, to the fact that I don't believe, in the future, we will consider the use of AI to be plagiarism at all.

Plagiarism has typically been thought to be the act of representing someone else's work as your own without attribution. There is also a lesser-known concept of self-plagiarism, which is reusing one's own work from the past and representing it as new work (often for credit in a class).

Let me repeat with emphasis: plagiarism is using someone *else's* work. Self-plagiarism is reusing one's *own* work.

In most definitions of plagiarism, the betrayal and deception concerning the agency of a *person* is the fundamental issue. It is taking the work a human has produced and passing it off as one's current work. And while we have rushed forward into the conclusion that AI use constitutes plagiarism, we have never stopped to reflect on whether that is actually true. We've simply assumed it to be true, like we assume the presence of an apple in the Garden of Eden, though Scripture does not specify the fruit. By this definition, AI use may be considered plagiarism if

1. we credit AI with a degree of human agency it does not possess (which is what we are unintentionally doing at present), and

2. we change our common definition of plagiarism so as to include nonhuman creation (what is most likely to happen in the short-term future).

Yet we fail to see that AI use does not constitute plagiarism if

3. we do not change our common definition of plagiarism, and AI eventually becomes a widespread and natural part of the ideation and creation process (what I believe is most likely to happen in the long-term future).

The second option is undoubtedly the space into which we're moving at present. But it is worth pointing out how this has been as a result not of careful consideration of *why*, but of hastily stumbling into the conclusion in an effort to quickly respond to the widespread adoption of ChatGPT.

This seems largely inconsequential to us now, but if and when a singularity event occurs (a moment, as we previously discussed, at which AI establishes an intelligence power, and possibly a sentience, equal to or greater than the capabilities of a human), the implications of our current decisions regarding AI and plagiarism unwittingly set a precedence lending credibility to a future argument that AI should be granted "rights" over what it creates, or eventually even other rights normally granted to a person (e.g., voting).

This certainly sounds like a far-fetched idea, as though I should be writing these words adorned with a tin-foil hat and mumbling about chem-trails in the sky. And perhaps my mildly dystopian slippery slope won't come to fruition. But if nothing more it serves as a cautionary example of the potential unintended consequences of playing fast and loose with long-standing categories when attempting to make sense of technological innovation without considering the possible consequences. In fact, I would argue much of how the academy has approached the topic of AI has focused more on hasty policymaking than deeper existential questions of how to prepare students for an AI future. We would serve humankind much better by leaning into the latter rather than focusing on the former, as I firmly believe that the widespread use of AI is an inevitability like so many other technologies we take for granted today.

Ultimately, I believe that AI use in content ideation and creation will become so normalized so as not to be any different from the regular use of Microsoft Word or Google, thus the need to cite its use will be odd and out of place. But until then, one possible solution is to follow the example of the undergraduate institution where I serve as Dean of Digital Ministry programs, Ascent College. In their AI policy (which I did not write) they refer to the unattributed use of AI as being "equal to" plagiarism, and thus a violation of the student code of conduct. It associates the practice with plagiarism without calling it such, allowing it to still exist in a sort of "other than" category. This policy provides a helpful framework to categorize the attempt to pass off AI-generated content as one's own work to be academically dishonest yet distinct from plagiarism itself.

HOW TO USE AI RIGHTLY

The question remains, then, what can and should we do with AI today in higher education? While tremendous opportunities exist at the level of LMS development, these are generally outside of the control of any educator or student. That said, the use of AI in education can be highly beneficial today in a variety of ways. Here is a rapid-fire list of uses that should be standard practices in educational environments today, which professors should not only encourage, but require, so as to position our students for an AI future:

- Students should use generative AI tools like ChatGPT for organizing the outline of their paper. AI is especially effective in helping to craft a well-formed thesis (and even explain to a student how to do it) and construct an outline for a paper that follows that thesis (a weakness that remains one of the most common issues I find when grading).

- Similarly, professors should use AI to help organize the flow of a course. Often a course flow makes sense in the head of the educator but doesn't to the student. Or, after a course has been taught for years, it often becomes misaligned and disjointed as successive professors have added their own flavor to the course. AI can help to reconstruct a flow that realigns courses and creates a cohesive experience for the student. I myself have done this when remaking existing courses, uploading the syllabus into an LLM like ChatGPT and prompting it to restructure the flow of the course to meet the course objectives and description. While this will almost always require some human editing to fine-tune to one's desired specifications, I've found it to be a very helpful foundation to build upon.

- Both students and professors alike can source recommended material from generative AI. A prompt like, "give me the twenty most influential books on hesychastic prayer" will likely yield a reasonable starting point for an unfamiliar topic.

- AI is a great resource for explaining or synthesizing material that is difficult to understand. When I began teaching a class on contextual theology to undergrad students, I wanted to use the six models presented in Stephen Bevans's 1992 book *Models of Contextual Theology*. I thought it was a bit too heady for the required reading list but would make a great lecture, so I asked ChatGPT to help me contextualize the information to make it easier to understand. It did a far better job than I could have done on my own.

- Generative AI is unreliable when it comes to citing content correctly, but it is absolutely fantastic in the mechanics of citations. For anyone working with citations, AI can pull a list of sources and format them to the bibliographic style you need, organize them alphabetically, and more. It makes the bibliography generator feature of the popular citation management software Zotero look ancient.

- AI-powered tools like translators, speech to text, and more, can empower professors to more easily accommodate the needs of students with linguistic or accessibility barriers.

- AI tools function as fantastic editors, trimming content to required word counts, cleaning up for clarity. AI can also act as a critic. A student can upload a copy of their paper to their preferred AI tool and ask it to critique the paper as though they were a PhD-level educated academic in the relevant field. The AI will assess both the good and the bad, allowing the student a round of feedback to strengthen their paper before turning it in.

The list certainly could go on, including AI-powered video creation, transcriptions, scheduling, and more. But beyond the tips and tricks available to the learning process today, the posture is what is more important. In Christian higher education, we have a choice between approaching AI with a proactive intentionality instead of a resistant fear. Educators must adopt a posture that recognizes the use of AI as inevitable and seeks to prepare students to develop personal practices that employ it wisely. Simply banning its use will do a disservice to students as well as to the educator who does not hone the necessary discernment to identify unattributed AI use in the papers he or she grades. Education, *especially* Christian education, necessitates the practice of empowering students to thrive in the world in which they live with the information they've learned in our classes. For students today, this necessarily involves learning to use AI wisely.

11

PRINCIPLES AND PRACTICES OF MINISTRY AI

AS WE CONCLUDE OUR JOURNEY TOGETHER, I want to end with a series of guiding principles, both in the form of theological and ecclesiological affirmations that can serve as a helpful guidepost for how to think well about artificial intelligence (AI), and a series of reflective questions to consider as Christians look to employ AI tools in life and ministry. After that, I will briefly recommend several specific resources that I believe are helpful for ministries as AI continues to develop and become increasingly sophisticated and further integrated into human society. Finally, I will end with a concluding benediction with my hopes for you as you apply the principles of this book in your life. I will now turn to a series of affirmations about AI that are necessary for Christians to consider, both in our churches and in our personal lives.

AI DEALS IN KNOWLEDGE, HUMANS DEAL IN WISDOM

The distinction between dealing in knowledge and dealing in wisdom is essential for understanding how to use AI well. Knowledge deals primarily with the accumulation and management of facts, while wisdom deals with the development of sound judgment and discernment. AI has the profound capacity to source information at lightning speed. It will only grow in its capacity to steward human knowledge, and we will only become increasingly dependent on turning to AI for that knowledge (you already do, in fact, every time you ask Google how old Kevin Bacon is or ask your Alexa to convert grams to cups while you're baking in the kitchen).

It is critical to understand that if your vocation deals primarily with the dissemination of knowledge, you will be faced with the choice to learn to integrate AI into your workflow well or face extinction. Information became decentralized with the emergence of household use of the internet. With the emergence of mobile technology, information became democratized, giving every-one equal capacity not only to source information but also to create it. Now, as AI has the capacity to teach people new skills and distill complex concepts in ways that are understood by the masses, information will become simplified, de-"classifying" con-cepts once held by experts. To borrow a phrase we used to shout back at preachers in my Pentecostal upbringing, AI is going to "make it plain!"

AI's limitation is in the cultivation of wisdom—referring both to wisdom cultivated within the individual as well as to an indi-vidual's capacity to cultivate wisdom in someone else. This is an essentially human quality, the value of which has been lost in our modern penchant for haste and ease, as well as in our over-reliance on facts as arbiters of truth. But a focus on wisdom and virtue, learning how to impart it in the lives of others, is an es-sential enterprise we must take up.

AI STEWARDS CONTENT, HUMANS STEWARD PEOPLE

Similar to the knowledge-wisdom dichotomy, AI is excellent at the organization, curation, and dissemination of content, which is a space many churches feel a need to fill. Church leaders with whom I speak often convey a deep dissatisfaction with the content sources discipling the people in their churches—whether they be cable news pundits or celebrities on Instagram—and feel the need to match that content production to shape people into a more "biblical worldview." But the rat race of content production is exhausting and a bit of a distraction since content consumption is only one component of a person's spiritual formation.

AI does provide resources, offer education and training efficiently (and often for free). The human factor that must be maintained—and improved upon—is the stewardship of *people*. AI can "know" at a systematic-theological level that human beings are fashioned in the image of God and deeply loved by their Creator. But only a human can *know* another human at a soul level. If we're honest with ourselves, we live in a time where far too many churches have become consumed with numerical (and financial) growth and need to return to embracing people at a soul level. By that I do not mean that we treat people as "souls" in the faceless sense that we've talked about people in churches in the past (e.g., "hundreds of souls were saved at that evangelistic crusade"). But rather, church and ministry leaders must cultivate a deep conviction *within their own soul* for the proper stewardship of the people entrusted to them. As followers of the way of Jesus, we must embrace the use of AI for the stewardship of content so that we can be free and focused to steward the people in our lives as they deserve to be stewarded—that is, to be respected and to be treasured. We must recognize that mentorship, spiritual guidance, person-to-person formation—these are the tasks for the people of God in the age of AI. Regardless of whether we have recognized it or not, it has been our task all along.

AI ANALYZES TRENDS, HUMANS DISCERN CONTEXT

AI can sift through vast amounts of data to identify trends and patterns. It is a gift that we would do well to integrate into our lives. Not long ago, I took part in drafting the final sections of a large white paper, coalescing research done by multiple Christian scholars from around the world and integrating my own work into it. In the final section I needed to tie everything together, so I uploaded the draft to ChatGPT and prompted it to analyze the paper and identify themes pursuant to the goal of the paper. ChatGPT did in seconds what took me hours to do on another white paper I wrote the year before. It wasn't perfect—I changed some of it, adding my own and removing AI-identified themes that were outliers. But it was nonetheless impressive. ChatGPT, Claude, Google Gemini, and more possess excellent capabilities for the analysis of data and trends.

But they're limited in their ability to analyze context, both the context in which a phenomenon is taking place and *actual* cultural context. I prompted both ChatGPT and Claude, asking them each to create a contextual exegesis report of the city of Flint, Michigan. Discerning context is a process missiologists call "contextual exegesis," a process of discerning needs, opportunities, history, loves, idols, and more within a particular city, people group, or community.

ChatGPT did a poor job, sticking mostly to facts about Flint's history of deindustrialization, crime, and the lead-in-water crisis that began in 2015. Its recommendations for ministry were generic enough to apply to just about any other town in America. Claude did a better job, even recommending ministry best practices that I had not considered. As someone who (1) is a missiologist, (2) grew up in the city in question, and (3) planted a church in the city in question, that Claude was able to make recommendations I hadn't considered was a bit humbling.

But there remain contextual phenomena that, as an AI, Claude simply isn't capable of handling. It cannot discern the smells coming from The Torch tavern in Buckham Alley in downtown Flint or the "suspicious hopefulness" a Flint resident feels when a new business venture promises to bring high-paying jobs. It can't understand the particular unspoken cultural nuances that exist between the Mott Park and College-Cultural districts. It can't discern spiritual forces at work. It can't abide with a people. It can't hope. These are essential human gifts that can't be easily replaced by an algorithm. We use our senses, our intuition, our spiritual discernment, and sometimes just a gut feeling to understand the context in which something takes place or where someone lives. That is fundamentally, and uniquely, human.

AI PREDICTS NEEDS, HUMANS MEET NEEDS

AI can forecast community needs based on data, but it takes human compassion and presence to address those needs effectively. Certainly AI can address the actual fulfillment of a need, such as employing AI-powered farming equipment to alleviate the physical demands on an aging population of farmers. But there is also a degree to which we must examine and ask ourselves whether AI *should* be the one to meet a need. In removing the human touch, do I lose something essential? Do I rob the one meeting the need and the one having their need met of something powerful, exchanging it for something transactional?

I recently followed the men's fashion guru Derek Guy on X (@dieworkwear) who is an apologist for something of a bygone era where men had a personal (usually lifelong) relationship with a local tailor, who custom fit clothing intended to be worn for years. I found myself a bit unnerved at that, as I generally don't even go into a brick-and-mortar store to pick out clothing. I order it all from an app, it arrives on my doorstep, and the task of getting new clothes (one that I despise) has been fulfilled. But what Guy describes is something entirely different—a deeply personal working relationship with an expert in his field who lives in the same community. Sure, it takes more time to go to a tailor, and it can be more expensive than simply buying from an app.

But have I lost something in allowing an algorithm to replace a human relationship in this part of my life? I think so.

Like most people, I despise going to the doctor. It's such a process, copays feel like a scam, and it's annoying to me that I need to drive twenty minutes to physically stand before a doctor so that she can verify whatever sickness I already know I have, just so I can get a prescription to get penicillin from the pharmacy across the street from where I live. So as much as I can, I use apps like Doctor on Demand and Teladoc. But I realize that in doing so, I've also given up much of the personal relationship that is cultivated with a family physician—a relationship that, as it did in my family, can span multiple generations. In thinking about what we outsource to AI, especially as AI becomes increasingly capable of meeting human needs, we need to examine whether what we lose by looping our humanity out of the need-meeting endeavor is truly worth it.

AI FACILITATES COMMUNICATION, HUMANS BUILD RELATIONSHIPS

AI tools can streamline and automate communication channels, yet building and nurturing genuine relationships remain a distinctly human task. Healthy relationships mature through a rhythm of time and attentiveness which, despite our best efforts in this siloed, individualistic cultural moment, remains essential to human flourishing. In his work on blue zones—those pockets of communities around the world where people tend to live incredibly long lives—longevity researcher Dan Buettner identified human connection as one of the most significant contributors to long life.[1] Relationship is not a perk or side piece to our work or personal ambitions; it is essential to our existence, and we must be directly involved in the process of initiating, growing, and maintaining our relationships.

However, this doesn't mean that AI cannot help facilitate relationship. Algorithms have been used for years to match people on online dating apps like Tinder and Bumble. More recently, many of these platforms are further integrating AI into the process of helping people navigate some of the barriers at the beginning of the online dating process, including developing a good bio, helping people amp up their flirting came with AI-generated opening lines and responses, and even generating AI profile pictures.

Critics of this degree of AI involvement in the matchmaking process say that AI's involvement is deception, acting as a digital Cyrano de Bergerac and thus duping the hopeful match on the other side of the app into thinking his or her love prospect is more promising than he or she actually is. Proponents counter that criticism, noting that we have long depended on friends for counsel and suggestions on how to talk to a love interest.[2] (I myself did this when mustering the courage to tell Tara how I felt about her when we were in college.) Other apps, such as Keys AI, can integrate AI-powered keyboards right to your phone that suggest prompts to facilitate human communication.

But however right or wrong, AI *is* involved in facilitating relationship communication. The question we must ask ourselves is the extent to which this facilitation is simply a convenience (such as the predictive suggestions when you write an email on Gmail or Microsoft Outlook). Or is this facilitation robbing us of some of the skills developed through trial and error in human communication? I developed the "skill" (I use that word *very* loosely) to talk to Tara leading up to and early in our dating relationship in our twenties through the often-embarrassing trials and errors of talking to girls as a teenager. AI can only take that process so far, as I found when I downloaded RizzGPT to see if it would up my flirting game with my wife and found it to be too superficial to communicate with a woman with whom I've cultivated deep love for many years. At the end of the day, the human touch will always be essential for human relationship.

AI CURATES TRANSACTIONAL EXPERIENCES, HUMANS CURATE TRANSFORMATIONAL EXPERIENCES

AI can organize and present information effectively, but the creation of meaningful experiences and memories is the domain of human creativity, empathy, and intuition. For those of us who preach, AI can aid in the construction and development of a sermon (and I think it *should*). But if that sermon is not birthed in the deep unction of our soul, if it is not bathed in prayer, if sweat and tears are not shed, then why even bother delivering it at all? AI can facilitate the production of content that communicates knowledge of God, but only God's daughters and sons are invited into his presence, to sit at his table, to recline against his chest.

Far too often we equate discipleship with the flat assimilation of information. But as I have addressed within this book, the process of being formed by the Spirit into the image of Christ (2 Cor 3:18) necessitates transformational encounters with the living God. In our churches, if we do not steward the presence of God well—if we are not attentive to his leading, if we aren't sensitive to removing barriers that allow people to encounter him, and if we are too concerned with our planned schedule that we do not give space for the Spirit to operate on *his* schedule—then we are missing a crucial component of the human connection with the God who made us and calls us by name.

This list of questions is certainly not exhaustive but may help paint a picture of the reflective optimism that I sincerely hope Christians will embody as we think about integrating AI evermore in our personal lives, vocations, and ministries. We need not simply think directly *about* AI, but also *around, above,* and *below* AI. By *around* I mean that we must examine those things that integration touches, rather than simply whatever function the AI is intended to improve. Often the unobvious things in our lives that orbit a change are the collateral damage of that change, yet we often think only of the improvement of the process the change is intended to bring about.

By *above*, I refer to thinking of those things that are transcendent, theological, and eschatological. We must consider what the integration of new AI means for us as humans, what it says about our hope of the return of Christ, and what it says about what we think about God. By *below*, I mean to refer to those things or people that may be unintentionally disadvantaged, marginalized, silenced, hurt, or even oppressed by the emergence of a new technology. I came of age watching firsthand how the emergence of automation (and more than a fair share of outsourcing) in the automotive industry devastated the economies of Flint and Detroit—all in the name of progress. That doesn't mean that change is always bad in the long term (both Flint and, especially, Detroit have since diversified their economies and become Rust Belt hotspots for innovation), but the process between immediate change and long-term benefit is often paved with heartache. The church is the ideal place of ministry, education, provision, advocacy, and comfort in that process.

AI TRENDS AND TOOLS FOR MINISTRY LEADERS

Before I turn to a few closing thoughts, I want to highlight two promising trends in the use of ministry AI that warrant further reflection and innovation. Then I will recommend several practical AI tools that are helpful, not only for church ministry but for Christian life more broadly.

Marketing-oriented missiology. The first trend is the use of marketing principles for the purpose of evangelism. While Western evangelicalism's entanglement with consumeristic practices is much criticized (and rightly so), what I refer to is quite different. The so-named "church industrial complex" leverages marketing practices to entice would-be attenders by appealing to their appetites.[3] It trades the Great Tradition for gimmicks—sacredness for entertainment—in the name of getting people into the church doors and eventually onto the tithe roll.

This market-driven ecclesiology appeals to the desires of the individual and requires amassing resources to perpetuate its continued existence. This is, very much, *not* what I'm talking about when I talk about marketing-oriented missiology. Instead, marketing-oriented missiology leverages best practices of marketing (the Hook Model, pipeline marketing, etc.) for the purpose of identifying people already asking spiritual questions and seeking to respond to those questions. Rather than someone Googling "who was Jesus" and winding up on some random blog written by a one-semester Bible college dropout who now does tarot card readings out of his mother's basement, the seeker winds up engaging with answers that help, provide solutions, and—most importantly—point toward healthy Christian community.

Some of the most promising forms of marketing-oriented missiology leverage the power of AI algorithms, which assess local internet use traffic and identify felt needs and pain points in an area. A multitude of mission agencies and evangelistic organizations leverage this information to create contextually appropriate ad campaigns that discuss those issues (be they marriage problems, financial hardship, family strife, or simple general interest in the Bible or in Jesus). These ad campaigns, like any other well-designed form of digital marketing, have a pipeline: when the user clicks the ad it routes them to a landing page on a website. The website then offers to connect with a chat (the organizations I know mainly use human digital missionaries for these chats, but it is easy to see how bots like Bible.ai or Faith Assistant could be employed here). From these conversations, seekers are either recommended to a local physical church community or placed in a variety of virtual communities to talk about the faith (e.g., Zoom chats, WhatsApp threads, private Facebook groups, etc.). This is not only effective in generating spiritual conversations in the

Western post-Christian world, but it is one of the most effective means of reaching people in restricted access nations.

It would be relatively simple for a local church to replicate this model. For instance, a church leader could partner with any number of organizations that provide behavioral insights based on the internet usage patterns of individuals within the local vicinity of the church. Then, the church could create a series of digital marketing campaigns on Google and social media based off those insights. The ads could route people to related landing pages on the church website with an integrated AI bot (such as Faith Assistant) to triage interactions. The bot could then refer conversations as appropriate to church leaders for further faith conversations. This is so simple that not only could a *church* do this, but an ambitious Christian with a desire to reach people far from God in digital spaces could do it individually, *especially* if their local church had a vision to assist.

The biggest barrier toward action like this that I have unfortunately observed, is not technological. It is that many churches—many Christians—simply do not want to deal with the "mess" of peoples' lives, since it is most often people in times of crisis who turn to internet searches for spiritual conversations. If ever there was evidence of our deep need for reformation in North American Christianity, it is this.

For those looking for easy ways to get their church involved in digital evangelism, marketing-oriented missiology is about as simple as it gets. AI handles much of the preliminary work so the Christian can focus on being a friend, a nonanxious presence in the life of a seeker.

Algorithmic discipleship. A second area in which AI can provide significant assistance to ministries of all types is in the area of discipleship. Remember what we have discussed earlier— discipleship (i.e., spiritual formation, mentorship, etc.) is so much more than content consumption. *But* the integration of information and ideas *is* one part of the discipleship journey. For those who already use online platforms (or plan to), the integration of AI-powered solutions is essential, to assist in providing information to users that is hand-tailored to their unique needs and transcends issues of accessibility and language barriers. AI can assess user needs, measure growth (to an extent), recommend solutions, and more.

Jesus.net, for example, uses AI in their database management and analytics for its online discipleship platform. They created their own unique set of measurements against which user development is routinely measured through benchmark data captured as users engage the platform. Based on these benchmark responses, AI recommends content to individual users that seeks to address the areas where their growth may be lagging, ensuring a more well-rounded discipleship journey and avoiding a person wading through irrelevant or redundant content.

Local churches or Christian entrepreneurs may find a resource like Faith Assistant helpful as well. Designed specifically with ministry in mind, this AI resource indexes and recommends content (including sermons, blogs, Bible studies, upcoming events, and more). It will report (anonymously) trending topic interactions in the form of "topic clusters" (like a word cloud, but based off what users are asking for the most). This allows a website owner to ascertain themes and topics of the greatest importance to the people using the site. The same organization that built Faith Assistant also offers "Christian GPTs," large language model AI that allows organizations to train AI for more advanced uses.

Other resources. While an entire book could be devoted to recommending AI resources (though it would have a short shelf life!), I want to commend several that I currently use or that I find extremely promising. These can help not only in the creation and dissemination of content in online spaces, but also for personal work and life management at the onset of the AI explosion.

- Pulpit.ai: A resource to help pastors maximize the use of their sermons (or professors, digital missionaries, or Christian influencers with any long-form video content). Pulpit.ai will splice long-form video into reels for social media and create devotionals, social media posts, small group guides, blog posts, and more. While it won't write your sermon (nor should it), it will help you mine for "connective tissue"—illustrations, historical examples, and more that help bring sermons more life. It can free up a large amount of time and people power—with all hope, so that Christians can be free to pursue more meaningful, people-facing ministry work.

- Lilt: Lilt provides AI-powered translation services that keep human involvement in the most important parts, ensuring accuracy and reliability. There are, of course, scores of other translation AI available now. Ministries, influencers, and digital missionaries simply must avail themselves of these resources. If you can potentially impact a couple billion more people simply by running content through a translation software that dubs your video or translates your written text into Mandarin or Farsi, why not?

- Custom GPTs: Using the premium plan for OpenAI's ChatGPT, users have the ability to create custom GPTs for specific projects, scopes of assistance, or particular purposes. The user can feed the custom GPT with the relevant data, both from the web or via file upload. I've created custom GPTs that function in a variety of helpful ways: a health, nutrition, and fitness coach; a course-designing assistant (for when I create new courses for a variety of college programs); a writing and research assistant (which has read nearly everything I've ever written and understands my voice and ideological commitments); and more. The possibilities of how custom GPTs are used are limited only by our imaginations.

- Claude: Similar to ChatGPT, Anthropic's Claude is a large language model AI that can perform a wide variety of functions. While not as widely known, Claude has advantages over ChatGPT, especially when it comes to research and writing. Popular LLMs like Chat, Claude, and Gemini will undoubtedly fight for "top dog" in any number of benchmarks in the years to come, but Claude is a valuable alternative, especially for those who are using free versions of each that limit the number of uses.

- Motion and ClickUp: If you're like me, you're on an eternal quest to find the right project and life management solution, and none of them seem to take the cake (or if you're like my wife, a piece of paper, a pen, and a good memory do just fine). But two AI-integrated productivity solutions that I find very helpful are Motion and ClickUp. Motion is an AI-powered project management software that integrates into most major calendar software programs and auto-schedules your work in the white space around your calendar. You can set the parameters of when and how work is prioritized and scheduled, and the integrated AI will automatically re-schedule any undone work and notify you if the reshuffling will result in anything going beyond its deadline. ClickUp doesn't have as powerful of a calendar-project integration but leverages AI within the projects itself. It is an all-in-one sort of workspace where AI can generate written content and automated workflows can bounce projects between team members, and more. Motion and ClickUp are two AI-powered life management solutions that are some of the best out there today.

QUESTIONS TO CONSIDER

Whether you are in vocational ministry or the marketplace, consider the following questions when you are discerning how to

effectively and wisely integrate AI into your own life, your
business, or your church, or in deciding to advocate for or against
the use of an AI in your community.

- How does integrating this AI tool reflect my understanding
  that people are made in the image of God?
- Does this AI perpetuate or exacerbate existing social inequalities? How does it help me hear voices I would not
  normally hear?
- How does engagement with this AI help me cultivate wisdom and virtue?
- How might this AI tool affect my relationships and community life, and how can I navigate these changes faithfully? What do I lose in my life, family, vocation, or ministry
  by integrating this resource? Is it worth that loss?
- How does this AI impact God's good creation (in its use of
  energy, in its capacity to exploit or improve, etc.)?
- How can I exercise a prophetic voice in critiquing and
  guiding the use of this AI tool? What are the impacts that
  are not being talked about?
- What can I do with this AI to promote transparency, accountability, privacy, and security?
- How might this AI tool influence my spiritual and moral
  formation, for the good or for the bad?
- What does my use of this resource say about what I believe
  about the hope of new creation?
- Does this fit within the ethics of the coming kingdom?

CONCLUSION

When we talk about digital technologies, three primary values
are always underpinning our conversations: (1) speed, (2) smartness, and (3) connectivity.[4] We value technology that is faster
than before. We value technology that can do more than before.

And we value technology that promises us greater connectivity than before. Undergirding these values is the promise that if greater speed, smartness, and connectivity is achieved, life will likely be better than it was before.

As the church, Christ's living embodiment on the earth in the age of artificial intelligence, we have the choice to continue to adopt these values as our own. Our pace of life can continue to increase. Our obsession with content-oriented discipleship and programmatic ministry can continue to dominate our approach to spiritual formation. Our constant availability and interconnectivity can erode our soul's need for deep reflection and mindfulness with the Lord. I'm convinced that this is not the vision for when AI goes to church. I'm convinced there's a different way— one that doesn't reject the potential of AI but also doesn't subjugate our values to it.

The future I long to see for the church is not one where Christians leverage new technologies to optimize and streamline their lives. It is not a future where increased speed makes way for increased toil, where the promise of heightened knowledge is a substitute for godly wisdom, or where connectivity is a cheap substitute for connection—with God and with one another.

Instead, the future I long to see is one that calls to mind the pace of the "three mile an hour God."[5] That is, while the world runs faster and faster, we would learn to walk at the pace of Jesus. We would adopt his more intentional, contemplative, and deliberate pace as we engage with humanity. If the future promises us efficiency with AI-optimized lives, may we prioritize personal presence and prayerful contemplation in our actions. May we learn to minister a bit more like monks and a little bit less like frantic stockbrokers.

The future I long to see is one where God's people steward AI to manage and interpret knowledge in concert with recapturing a hunger for godly wisdom. If the future promises us all of the world's knowledge at our fingertips, then may we be a shining city on a hill example of what it means to tell truth from error, exercise Spirit-led discernment, and advocate for a more righteous and equitable society as a foretaste of the coming kingdom.

The future I long to see is one where God's people steward AI in such a way that it makes space in our lives for deeper human-to-human connection. If the future promises us humanoid robots who can cook and clean for us, then by all means let's use that freed time for meaningful dialogue with our spouse and children, to make music and art, to write poetry, to bake a pie for our neighbor, to plant a community garden, or to volunteer at a senior center. Let our AI future break us free from the shackles of outdated approaches to work and call us toward something meaningful and people-prioritizing.

I can't say for certain what artificial intelligence will look like in the future. But I can with certainty say that God's mission for the church in the world remains unchanged: to carry the good news of the risen one who took on flesh and dwelt among us, promising to one day come again.

EPILOGUE

We have the opportunity to get ahead in the process of theologizing artificial intelligence (AI) well in a way that we did not do in the emergence of smartphones and mobile technology. Pastors everywhere are struggling with how to reactively respond to issues created by these technologies, such as isolation, expressive individualism, ideological radicalization, anxiety, depression, and suicidal ideation (especially among youth). And while some of these phenomena were unavoidable, I do wonder whether, had we taken more time at the emergence of these technologies to wrap our heads around the possibilities and pitfalls of such a powerful technology, we would be better positioned to respond to the issues at hand. AI and the emergence of other Web 3.0 technologies present a similar dilemma before us. The question is not *if* it will change us in ways we cannot anticipate, the question is *when* and *how*. And we must do better at thinking critically about AI than we did mobile technology at its genesis. We can better prepare the generations that follow us for an AI future better than we prepared young Millennials and elder Gen Z for the smartphone boom. But we must begin that reflection and dialogue now.

I conclude this journey deeply encouraged, not only because of how AI can reshape the world for the better, but because once you turn down the volume of sensationalism that surrounds the cultural conversation about AI, you find that the same still small voice that called out to Elijah continues to speak to the people of God in the age of AI. Regardless of what innovation, progress, or crises befall humanity, we remain the beloved daughters and sons of a God who knows us each by name. He is the same God who stepped into the brokenness of this world in the God-man Jesus the Messiah to reconcile people far from him. He is the same God who, through his Son, is remaking the world and has given us the hope of a future created order in which every injustice has been made righteous, every pain healed, every tear wiped away. The refugee will find shelter. Empires will fall. Death will be no more. Peace will reign forever. Whether or not some version of a redeemed AI is a part of that new created order is unknown. But what *is* known is the unshakable, irrevocable assurance that he is our God, and we are his people (Ex 6:7; Rev 21:3).

> O be joyful in the LORD, all you lands;
>> Serve the LORD with gladness, and come before his
>>> presence with a song.
> Be assured that the LORD, he is God;
>> it is he that has made us, and not we ourselves;
>> we are his people, and the sheep of his pasture.
> O go your way into his gates with thanksgiving, and into his
>> courts with praise;
>> be thankful unto him, and speak good of his Name.
> For the LORD is gracious, his mercy is everlasting,
>> and his truth endures from generation to generation.
>
> Psalm 100, Book of Common Prayer, Anglican Church of North America

ACKNOWLEDGMENTS

The Rev. Dr. Tara Korpi is not only my wife but also my dearest friend and a faithful pastor and semiotician. I'm thankful for her ongoing support in my writing, in ministry, and in life. Tara, God has blessed me with a lot, but you surpass it all.

Ed Stetzer, who is not only a best-in-class example of what it means to make missiology accessible for everyone, but whose integrity and consistency is a breath of fresh air. Tara and I are both grateful not only for the doors he has opened for us over the years but also for his mentorship and friendship.

Rob Hoskins is one of the best leaders and thinkers I know, proving through his leadership of OneHope that a ministry can be innovative, healthy, effective, and true to its calling. His leadership and encouragement give me a vision to which I can aspire. Thank you for everything, Rob, as well as to David Branker, Jenn Brown, and the rest of the OneHope family.

I would like to thank my literary agent, Keely Boeving, for your encouragement, feedback, professionalism, and commitment to helping me make my work the best it can be. Al Hsu, who is the editor for this book, and the rest of the InterVarsity Press team have been an absolute joy to work with. I couldn't have found a better home for this work. I'm very grateful.

NOTES

1. A BRAVE NEW WORLD

[1] Michael and Denise Okuda, "From the Star Trek Archive: Communicators and PADDS," StarTrek.com, June 18, 2024, www.startrek.com /gallery/star-trek-archive-okudagrams.

[2] Associated Press "Fusion Breakthrough Means 'Basically Unlimited' Fuel Is Now a Possibility," Fox2 Detroit, December 13, 2022, https://tinyurl .com/4vxuzjzr.

[3] Apple Support, "Use Live Listen with AirPods or Beats," Apple Support, October 4, 2023, https://tinyurl.com/2wr2vesf.

[4] Emily Witt, "The Future of Fertility," *The New Yorker*, April 17, 2023, www.newyorker.com/magazine/2023/04/24/the-future-of-fertility.

[5] A missiologist is an academic who teaches, studies, and writes on Christianity's engagement with culture, especially as it concerns communicating and embodying the gospel.

[6] Henry Kissinger et al., *The Age of AI: And Our Human Future* (New York, NY: Little, Brown, 2021), 181.

[7] See Ralph D. Winter, "The Two Structures of God's Redemptive Mission," in *Perspectives on the World Christian Movement: A Reader* by Ralph D. Winter et al. (Princeton, NJ: William Carey Publishing, 2009), 244-53.

[8] Justin Wise, *The Social Church: A Theology of Digital Communication* (Chicago: Moody Publishers, 2014), 111.

[9] "2024 Largest Participating Churches," Outreach 100, https://tinyurl .com/4ch5ey96; Leonardo Blair, "I Went to Church in the Metaverse and This Is What I Found," *The Christian Post*, June 2, 2022, https://tinyurl .com/3w3rz2m6.

[10] Julie Anne Lytle, *Faith Formation 4.0: Introducing an Ecology of Faith in a Digital Age* (New York: Morehouse, 2013), 72.

[11] Genevieve Bell, "The Boyer Lectures 2017: Fast, Smart and Connected: What Is It to Be Human, and Australian, in a Digital World?" (ABC Audio, 2017), 31:00-33:00, Audible.

[12] See https://tinyurl.com/3jcdh2ba.

2. UNDERSTANDING ARTIFICIAL INTELLIGENCE

[1]Henry Kissinger et al., *The Age of AI: And Our Human Future* (New York: Little, Brown, 2021), 55.

[2]Kissinger et al., *Age of AI*, 55.

[3]Kavita Ganesan, *The Business Case for AI: A Leader's Guide to AI Strategies, Best Practices & Real-World Applications* (Sandy, UT: Opinosis Analytics, 2022), 15.

[4]IBM Data and AI Team, "Understanding the Different Types of Artificial Intelligence," IBM.com, October 12, 2023, https://tinyurl.com/2ved4vu4.

[5]*Creeped Out*, season 2 episode 3, "Help," written by Robert Butler and Stephen Cooke, directed by Bruce McDonald, aired May 8, 2019, on Netflix.

[6]Kissinger et al., *Age of AI*, 55.

[7]Genevieve Bell, "The Boyer Lectures 2017: Fast, Smart and Connected: What Is It to Be Human, and Australian, in a Digital World?" (ABC Audio, 2017), 31:00-33:00, Audible.

[8]Rockwell Anyoha, "The History of Artificial Intelligence," Harvard Graduate School of Arts and Sciences, August 28, 2017, https://sites.harvard.edu/sitn/2017/08/28/history-artificial-intelligence/.

[9]Kissinger et al., *Age of AI*, 60.

[10]BBC News, "Google AI Defeats Human Go Champion," BBC.com, May 25, 2017, www.bbc.com/news/technology-40042581.

[11]Kissinger et al., *Age of AI*, 58; David Silver et al., "Mastering Chess and Shogi by Self-Play with a General Reinforcement Learning Algorithm," arXiv, Cornell University, December 5, 2017, https://tinyurl.com/2t8pp8f6.

[12]For more see Michael S. Heiser, *The Unseen Realm: Recovering the Supernatural Worldview of the Bible* (Bellingham, WA: Lexham Press, 2015), chap. 11; John H. Walton, *The Lost World of Adam and Eve: Genesis 2–3 and the Human Origins Debate* (Downers Grove, IL: IVP Academic, 2015), 116-38; Jean Chevalier and Alain Gheerbrant, *A Dictionary of Symbols*, trans. John Buchanan-Brown (London, UK: Penguin Books, 1996), 844-58; John H. Walton, Victor H. Matthews, and Mark W. Chavalas, *The IVP Bible Background Commentary: Old Testament* (Downers Grove, IL: InterVarsity Press, 2000), 31-32.

[13]For greater exposition on the elimination of patriarchy, see Todd Korpi, *Your Daughters Shall Prophesy: Amplifying the Voice and Place of Christian Women* (Eugene, OR: Wipf & Stock, 2023), 14-15.

3. SCRIPTURE AND THE CHALLENGE
OF MODERN TECHNOLOGY

[1]John Walton is likely the most notable originator of this sentiment: "The Old Testament *does* communicate to us and it was written for us, and for all humankind. But it was not written *to* us. It was written to Israel." See John Walton, *The Lost World of Genesis One: Ancient Cosmology and the Origins Debate* (Downers Grove, IL: IVP Academic, 2009), 7.

[2]Jonathan Haidt, *The Anxious Generation* (New York: Penguin Press, 2024), 26-27.

[3]Haidt, *Anxious Generation*, 28-29.

[4]Paul Hiebert, *Transforming Worldviews: An Anthropological Understanding of How People Change* (Grand Rapids, MI: Baker Academic, 2008), 26-27.

[5]J. de Waal Dryden, *A Hermeneutic of Wisdom: Recovering the Formative Agency of Scripture* (Grand Rapids, MI: Baker Academic, 2018), 19-20.

[6]Dryden, *Hermeneutic of Wisdom*, xx-xxi.

4. AI AND THE IMAGE OF GOD

[1]A. Scott Moreau, *Contextualizing the Faith: A Holistic Approach* (Grand Rapids, MI: Baker Academic, 2018), 101.

[2]Paul G. Hiebert, R. Daniel Shaw, and Tite Tiénou, *Understanding Folk Religion: A Christian Response to Popular Beliefs and Practices* (Grand Rapids, MI: Baker Books, 1999), 260-62.

[3]Hiebert, Shaw, and Tiénou, *Understanding Folk Religion*, 254.

[4]On Shelley as a foundation for media depictions of AI see Lucas Duncan, "Body, Mind, Soul—The 'Cyborg Effect': Artificial Intelligence in Science Fiction" (master's thesis, Hamilton, Ontario, McMaster University, 2002).

[5]For more on Acts as a "prophetic" history, see Luke Timothy Johnson, *Prophetic Jesus, Prophetic Church: The Challenge of Luke-Acts to Contemporary Christians* (Grand Rapids, MI: Eerdmans, 2011).

[6]John H. Walton, *The Lost World of Genesis One: Ancient Cosmology and the Origins Debate* (Downers Grove, IL: IVP Academic, 2009), 15.

[7]Todd Korpi, *Your Daughters Shall Prophesy: Amplifying the Voice and Place of Christian Women* (Eugene, OR: Wipf & Stock, 2023), 11.

[8]Walton, *Lost World of Genesis One*, 21; Carmen Joy Imes, *Being God's Image: Why Creation Still Matters*, (Downers Grove, IL: IVP Academic, 2023), 35.

[9]John H. Walton, Victor H. Matthews, and Mark W. Chavalas, *The IVP Bible Background Commentary: Old Testament* (Downers Grove, IL: InterVarsity Press, 2000), 29.

[10]Imes, *Being God's Image*, 35.

[11]Michael S. Heiser, *The Unseen Realm: Recovering the Supernatural Worldview of the Bible* (Bellingham, WA: Lexham Press, 2015), 40-41.

[12]Johnson Space Center Office of Communications, "NASA Humanoid Robot to Be Tested in Australia," NASA.gov, July 6, 2023, www.nasa.gov/centers-and-facilities/johnson/nasa-humanoid-robot-to-be-tested-in-australia/.

[13]"Replika," replika.com, accessed July 18, 2023, https://replika.com.

[14]"This App Is Trying to Replicate You," *Quartz*, August 29, 2019, https://tinyurl.com/5b965jrt.

[15]Erin Nolan, "For Older People Who Are Lonely, Is the Solution a Robot Friend?," *The New York Times*, July 6, 2024, https://tinyurl.com/yckjp5sx.

[16]Charlotte Edwards, "The Smell of Your Freshly Cut Lawn Is Grass 'Screaming' to Warn Other Plants They're under Attack," News.com.au, October 7, 2019, https://tinyurl.com/2h9e8wr8.

[17]Andy Crouch, *Culture Making: Recovering Our Creative Calling* (Downers Grove, IL: InterVarsity Press, 2008), 17-25.

[18]"Incident 266: Replika's 'AI Companions' Reportedly Abused by Its Users," AI Incident Database, n.d., https://tinyurl.com/yhjyzuxa.

[19]Bernard Rollin, "Animal Ethics and the Law," *Michigan Law Review First Impressions* 106, no. 1 (2008), https://tinyurl.com/56s35mw7.

5. AI THEOLOGY AND ETHICS

[1]J. de Waal Dryden, *A Hermeneutic of Wisdom: Recovering the Formative Agency of Scripture* (Grand Rapids, MI: Baker Academic, 2018), 47-48.

[2]Dryden, *Hermeneutic of Wisdom*, 42.

[3]Dryden, *Hermeneutic of Wisdom*, 36.

[4]Wendell Berry, *The World Ending Fire: The Essential Wendell Berry* (Berkeley, CA: Counterpoint, 2017), 167-68.

[5]Berry, *World Ending Fire*, 172.

[6]N. T. Wright, *Surprised by Hope* (San Francisco: HarperOne 2008), 265-66.

[7]Andy Crouch, *Culture Making: Recovering Our Creative Calling* (Downers Grove, IL: InterVarsity Press, 2008), 216.

[8]Todd Korpi, *Your Daughters Shall Prophesy: Amplifying the Voice and Place of Christian Women* (Eugene, OR: Wipf & Stock, 2023), 39-51.

[9]Berry, *World Ending Fire*, 235.

[10]Berry, *World Ending Fire*, 235.

[11]Peter Block, Walter Brueggemann, and John McKnight, *An Other Kingdom: Departing the Consumer Culture* (Hoboken, NJ: Wiley, 2016), 26-27.

[12]Makoto Fujimura, *Culture Care: Reconnecting with Beauty for Our Common Life* (Downers Grove, IL: InterVarsity Press, 2017), 34.

[13]For more, see Matthew W. Bates, *Salvation by Allegiance Alone: Rethinking Faith, Works, and the Gospel of Jesus the King* (Grand Rapids, MI: Baker Academic, 2017).

[14]Paul Hiebert, *Transforming Worldviews: An Anthropological Understanding of How People Change* (Grand Rapids, MI: Baker Academic, 2008), 291.

[15]Block, Brueggemann, and McKnight, *Other Kingdom*, 68.

6. AI AND THE MISSION OF THE CHURCH

[1]For a deeper explanation of signs and symbols in human communication, see Paul G. Hiebert, R. Daniel Shaw, and Tite Tiénou, *Understanding Folk Religion: A Christian Response to Popular Beliefs and Practices* (Grand Rapids, MI: Baker Books, 1999), 231-55.

[2]"51% of Churchgoers Don't Know of the Great Commission," Barna Group, March 27, 2018, https://tinyurl.com/594c4bfe.

[3]Ralph D. Winter et al., *Perspectives on the World Christian Movement: A Reader* (Princeton, NJ: William Carey Publishing, 2009), 367.

[4]Charles Van Engen, *God's Missionary People: Rethinking the Purpose of the Local Church* (Grand Rapids, MI: Baker Book House, 1991), 109-12; Todd Korpi, "A Holy Priesthood: Cultivating Ecosystems for Missional Formation at Celebration Church" (DMiss. diss., Fuller Theological Seminary, 2022), 31-33.

[5]Korpi, "Holy Priesthood," 27-37.

[6]Bengt Sundkler, *The World of Mission*, Foundations of Mission Series (Grand Rapids, MI: Eerdmans, 1965).

[7]Winter et al., *Perspectives on the World Christian Movement*, 244-53.

[8]Kimberly Gedeon, "Microsoft Edge Will Use AI to Add Real-Time Translation to Videos—What This Means for You," Mashable, May 21, 2024, https://tinyurl.com/2uwhj4jj.

[9]Todd Korpi, "The Digital Frontier of Mission," Digital Mission Consortia (Wheaton, IL: Wheaton College Billy Graham Center, June 2023), 24-25, 34.

[10]Korpi, "Holy Priesthood," 67-71.

[11]Korpi, "Holy Priesthood," 64-71.

7. AI AND SOCIAL JUSTICE

[1]Vera Bergengruen, "The War Lab," *Time*, February 26, 2024, 30-35.

[2]Bergengruen, "War Lab," 30. "Mil" is a shortened form of "military."

[3]Bergengruen, "War Lab," 30.

[4]Bergengruen, "War Lab," 31.

[5]Bergengruen, "War Lab," 35.

[6]David González, "Laguna Beach HS Investigating Incident Involving AI-Generated Nude Photos of Students," *ABC7*, April 1, 2024, https://tinyurl.com/34ykvm59; Sid Garcia, "5 Beverly Hills Students Expelled for Sharing AI-Generated Nudes of Classmates," *ABC7*, March 8, 2024, https://tinyurl.com/3bed4w7h; Riana Pfefferkorn, "Teens Are Spreading Deepfake Nudes of One Another. It's No Joke," *Scientific American*, June 10, 2024, https://tinyurl.com/mwu5syn4; Natasha Singer, "Teen Girls Confront an Epidemic of Deepfake Nudes in Schools," *The New York Times*, April 8, 2024, https://tinyurl.com/32th84sc.

[7]World Health Organization, "The True Death Toll of Covid-19: Estimating Global Excess Mortality," May 20, 2021, https://tinyurl.com/mrcem76c.

[8]Lesslie Newbigin, *The Gospel in a Pluralist Society* (Grand Rapids, MI: Eerdmans, 1989), 135.

[9]Newbigin, *Gospel in a Pluralist Society*, 136-39.

[10]Tom Boellstorff et al., *Data, Now Bigger and Better!* (Chicago, IL: Prickly Paradigm Press, 2015), 1.

[11]Boellstorff et al., *Data, Now*, 11-12.

[12]Boellstorff et al., *Data, Now*, 13.

[13]Boelstorff et al., *Data, Now*, 17-18.

[14]Jeffrey Dastin, "Insight—Amazon Scraps Secret AI Recruiting Tool That Showed Bias Against Women," *Reuters* (blog), October 10, 2018, https://tinyurl.com/yt4javy5.

[15]Jeff Larson et al., "How We Analyzed the COMPAS Recidivism Algorithm," *ProPublica*, May 23, 2016, https://tinyurl.com/3ztpjd28.

[16]Alyxaundria Sanford, "Artificial Intelligence Is Putting Innocent People at Risk of Being Incarcerated," *Innocence Project*, February 14, 2014, https://tinyurl.com/3zhyjmdt.

17James Vincent, "Twitter Taught Microsoft's AI Chatbot to Be a Racist Asshole in Less than a Day," *The Verge*, March 24, 2016, https://tinyurl.com/4au4fwbz.

18Vincent, "Twitter Taught."

19Melissa Heikkilä, "How It Feels to Be Sexually Objectified by an AI," *MIT Technology Review*, December 13, 2022, https://tinyurl.com/5vfpu92e.

20Gianluca Mauro and Hilke Schellmann, "'There Is No Standard': Investigation Finds AI Algorithms Objectify Women's Bodies," *The Guardian*, February 8, 2023, https://tinyurl.com/4kpuyztb.

21IBM Data and AI Team, "Shedding Light on AI Bias with Real World Examples," IBM.com, October 16, 2023, https://tinyurl.com/55nenfhc.

22Genevieve Bell, "The Boyer Lectures 2017: Fast, Smart and Connected: What Is It to Be Human, and Australian, in a Digital World?" (ABC Audio, 2017), Audible.

23Bell, "Boyer Lectures 2017," chap. 4.

24Emma Korynta, "'Art Will Never Be the Same:' Charlotte Artist Has Her Work Scraped by AI," WCNC Charlotte, December 20, 2023, https://tinyurl.com/yc74hha7.

25Mary Rasenberger, "Opinion: As AI Is Embraced, What Happens to the Artists Whose Work Was Stolen to Build It'" *Los Angeles Times*, June 18, 2024, https://tinyurl.com/4msnfxkt.

26Bell, "Boyer Lectures 2017," chap. 4.

27Wendell Berry, *The World Ending Fire: The Essential Wendell Berry* (Berkeley, CA: Counterpoint, 2017), 55.

28Berry, *World Ending Fire*, 53.

8. AI AND THE FUTURE OF WORK

1Jennifer Latson, "When Daylight Saving Time Was Year-Round," *Time*, February 9, 2015, https://time.com/3695333/daylight-saving-time-wwii/.

2As quoted in Pekka Himanen, *The Hacker Ethic and the Spirit of the Information Age* (New York: Random House, 2001), 34.

3Himanen, *Hacker Ethic*, 34-37.

4Himanen, *Hacker Ethic*, 36.

5Marguerite Ward, "A Brief History of the 8-Hour Workday, Which Changed How Americans Work," *CNBC*, May 3, 2017, https://tinyurl.com/6muna3t2.

6Himanen, *Hacker Ethic*, 107.

[7]Himanen, *Hacker Ethic*, 26.

[8]*Dumb and Dumber* Quotes, IMDb, accessed February 10, 2025, www.imdb.com/title/tt0109686/quotes/.

[9]"The Productivity-Pay Gap," *Economic Policy Institute*, October 2022, updated December 2024, https://tinyurl.com/esz8kbun.

[10]Charlie Giattino, Esteban Ortiz-Ospina, and Max Roser, "Working Hours," *Our World in Data*, 2020, https://ourworldindata.org/working-hours.

[11]"The Top 10 Largest Economies in the World in 2025," *Forbes India*, January 10, 2025, www.forbesindia.com/article/explainers/top-10-largest-economies-in-the-world/86159/1.

[12]Andrea Hsu, "Iceland Cut Its Workweek and Found Greater Happiness and No Loss in Productivity," *NPR*, July 6, 2021, https://tinyurl.com/2efsjpwr.

[13]Giulia Carbonaro, "Is the 6-Hour Workday the Answer to a Better Work-Life Balance?," *Euro News*, July 27, 2022, https://tinyurl.com/4funymzu; Steve Glaveski, "The Case for the 6-Hour Workday," *Harvard Business Review*, December 11, 2018, https://tinyurl.com/mvucx8ae.

[14]Bruce Philip, "Marxism, Neoclassical Economics and the Length of the Working Day," *Review of Political Economy* 13, no. 1 (January 1, 2001): 27-39, https://doi.org/10.1080/09538250150210568.

[15]Himanen refers to this construct as the "Protestant work ethic" because of its emergence paralleled the Protestant Reformation and has been a feature common within the work ethic of the Protestant world. He makes this association *historically,* not *theologically.* Himanen, *Hacker Ethic*, 43.

[16]Himanen, *Hacker Ethic*, 33.

[17]Antonio Spadaro and Maria Way, *Cybertheology: Thinking Christianity in the Era of the Internet* (New York: Fordham University Press, 2014), 54.

[18]Caleb J. Lines, *The Great Digital Commission: Embracing Social Media for Church Growth and Transformation* (Eugene, OR: Cascade Books, 2021), 36.

9. PASTORAL CARE AND ARTIFICIAL CLERGY

[1]"Occupational Employment and Wage Statistics," *U.S. Bureau of Labor Statistics*, May 2023, https://tinyurl.com/54vak9uf.

[2]Samuel R. Chand, *Leadership Pain: The Classroom for Growth* (Nashville: Thomas Nelson, 2015), 35.

[3]Sara Billups, *Orphaned Believers: How a Generation of Christian Exiles Can Find the Way Home* (Grand Rapids, MI: Baker Books, 2023), 14.

[4]Dhruv Khullar, "Talking to Ourselves." *The New Yorker*, March 6, 2023, 16-22.

[5]Khullar, "Talking to Ourselves," 17.

[6]See Henri J. M. Nouwen, *Reaching Out: The Three Movements of the Spiritual Life* (Garden City, NY: Doubleday, 1975).

[7]Khullar, "Talking to Ourselves," 17.

[8]Todd Korpi, "The Digital Frontier of Mission," Digital Mission Consortia (Wheaton, IL: Wheaton College Billy Graham Center, June 2023), 15.

[9]Todd Korpi, "Renovating Pastoring," *Church Talk with Todd Korpi* (blog), September 21, 2023, https://toddkorpi.substack.com/p/renovating -pastoring.

10. AI AND CHRISTIAN HIGHER EDUCATION

[1]Michelle Harwood, "AI Wrote the US Constitution, Says AI Content Detector," *Medium*, September 7, 2023, https://tinyurl.com/2f9b4d9c.

[2]Turnitin, "AI Writing," https://tinyurl.com/y9y7wkye.

[3]Patricia Armstrong, "Bloom's Taxonomy," Vanderbilt University, 2010, https://tinyurl.com/mrxzrem4.

[4]Dallas Willard, *Renovation of the Heart: Putting on the Character of Christ* (Colorado Springs: NavPress, 2002), 39-40.

[5]Jane Kathryn Vella, *Learning to Listen, Learning to Teach: The Power of Dialogue in Educating Adults*, rev. ed., Jossey-Bass Higher and Adult Education Series (San Francisco: Jossey-Bass, 2002), 4.

[6]Heidi Campbell and John Dyer, eds., *Ecclesiology for a Digital Church: Theological Reflections on a New Normal* (London: SCM Press, 2021), 82.

11. PRINCIPLES AND PRACTICES OF MINISTRY AI

[1]Dan Buettner, "Power 9®: Reverse Engineering Longevity," *Blue Zones*, accessed February 10, 2025, www.bluezones.com/2016/11/power-9.

[2]Britnei Bilhete, "From AI Dating to Flirt Coaches: How AI Is Changing Dating, for Better or Worse," *CBC*, March 22, 2024, https://tinyurl.com /bdfsapmr.

[3]J. R. Woodward and Dan White Jr., *The Church as Movement: Starting and Sustaining Missional-Incarnational Communities* (Downers Grove, IL: InterVarsity Press, 2016), 24-26.

[4]Genevieve Bell, "The Boyer Lectures 2017: Fast, Smart and Connected: What Is It to Be Human, and Australian, in a Digital World?" (ABC Audio, 2017), Audible.

[5]See Kosuke Koyama's *Three Mile an Hour God* (London: SCM,1979).

WORKS CITED

"2024 Largest Participating Churches." Outreach 100, n.d. https://tinyurl .com/4ch5ey96.

AI Incident Database. "Incident 266: Replika's 'AI Companions' Reportedly Abused by Its Users," n.d. https://tinyurl.com/yhjyzuxa.

Anyoha, Rockwell. "The History of Artificial Intelligence." *Harvard Graduate School of Arts and Sciences* (blog), August 28, 2017. https:// sites.harvard.edu/sitn/2017/08/28/history-artificial-intelligence.

Apple Support. "Use Live Listen with AirPods or Beats." Apple Support, October 4, 2023. https://tinyurl.com/2wr2vesf.

Armstrong, Patricia. "Bloom's Taxonomy." Vanderbilt University, 2010. https://tinyurl.com/mrxzrem4.

Associated Press. "Fusion Breakthrough Means 'Basically Unlimited' Fuel Is Now a Possibility." Fox2 Detroit, December 13, 2022. https://tinyurl .com/4vxuzjzr.

Barna Group. "51% of Churchgoers Don't Know of the Great Commission." March 27, 2018. https://tinyurl.com/594c4bfe.

Bates, Matthew W. *Salvation by Allegiance Alone: Rethinking Faith, Works, and the Gospel of Jesus the King.* Grand Rapids, MI: Baker Academic, 2017.

BBC News. "Google AI Defeats Human Go Champion." May 25, 2017. www .bbc.com/news/technology-40042581.

Bell, Genevieve. "The Boyer Lectures 2017: Fast, Smart and Connected: What Is It to Be Human, and Australian, in a Digital World?" ABC Audio, 2017. Audible.

Bergengruen, Vera. "The War Lab." *Time,* February 26, 2024.

Berry, Wendell. *The World Ending Fire: The Essential Wendell Berry.* Berkeley, CA: Counterpoint, 2017.

Bilhete, Britnei. "From AI Dating to Flirt Coaches: How AI Is Changing Dating, for Better or Worse." *CBC,* March 22, 2024. https://tinyurl .com/bdfsapmr.

Billups, Sara. *Orphaned Believers: How a Generation of Christian Exiles Can Find the Way Home.* Grand Rapids, MI: Baker Books, 2023.

Blair, Leonardo. "I Went to Church in the Metaverse and This Is What I Found." *The Christian Post*, June 2, 2022. https://tinyurl.com/3w3rz2m6.

Block, Peter, Walter Brueggemann, and John McKnight. *An Other Kingdom: Departing the Consumer Culture*. Hoboken, NJ: Wiley, 2016.

Boellstorff, Tom, Bill Maurer, Genevieve Bell, Melissa Gregg, and Nick Seaver. *Data, Now Bigger and Better!* Chicago, IL: Prickly Paradigm Press, 2015.

Buettner, Dan. "Power 9®: Reverse Engineering Longevity." *Blue Zones*, accessed February 10, 2025, www.bluezones.com/2016/11/power-9.

Campbell, Heidi, and John Dyer, eds. *Ecclesiology for a Digital Church: Theological Reflections on a New Normal*. London: SCM Press, 2021.

Carbonaro, Giulia. "Is the 6-Hour Workday the Answer to a Better Work-Life Balance?" *Euro News*, July 27, 2022. https://tinyurl.com/4funymzu.

The Center for Humane Technologies. "The Wisdom Gap," n.d. https://tinyurl.com/mrxrvau4.

Chand, Samuel R. *Leadership Pain: The Classroom for Growth*. Nashville: Thomas Nelson, 2015.

Chevalier, Jean, and Alain Gheerbrant. *A Dictionary of Symbols*. Translated by John Buchanan-Brown. London, UK: Penguin Books, 1996.

Chilcote, Paul Wesley, and Laceye C. Warner, eds. *The Study of Evangelism: Exploring a Missional Practice of the Church*. Grand Rapids, MI: Eerdmans, 2008.

Crouch, Andy. *Culture Making: Recovering Our Creative Calling*. Downers Grove, IL: InterVarsity Press, 2008.

Dastin, Jeffrey. "Insight—Amazon Scraps Secret AI Recruiting Tool That Showed Bias Against Women." *Reuters* (blog), October 10, 2018. https://tinyurl.com/yt4javy5.

Dryden, J. de Waal. *A Hermeneutic of Wisdom: Recovering the Formative Agency of Scripture*. Grand Rapids, MI: Baker Academic, 2018.

Duncan, Lucas. "Body, Mind, Soul—The 'Cyborg Effect': Artificial Intelligence in Science Fiction." MA Thesis, McMaster University, 2002.

Economic Policy Institute. "The Productivity-Pay Gap." October 2022, updated December 2024. https://tinyurl.com/esz8kbun.

Edwards, Charlotte. "The Smell of Your Freshly Cut Lawn Is Grass 'Screaming' to Warn Other Plants They're Under Attack." News.com.au, October 7, 2019. https://tinyurl.com/2h9e8wr8.

Ferguson, Trey. *Theologizin' Bigger: Homilies on Living Freely and Loving Wholly*. Grand Rapids, MI: Lake Drive Books, 2024.

Forbes India. "The Top 10 Largest Economies in the World in 2024." November 4, 2024. https://tinyurl.com/53mrfrmr.

Fujimura, Makoto. *Culture Care: Reconnecting with Beauty for Our Common Life.* Downers Grove, IL: InterVarsity Press, 2017.

Ganesan, Kavita. *The Business Case for AI: A Leader's Guide to AI Strategies, Best Practices & Real-World Applications.* Sandy, UT: Opinosis Analytics, 2022.

Garcia, Sid. "5 Beverly Hills Students Expelled for Sharing AI-Generated Nudes of Classmates." *ABC7,* March 8, 2024. https://tinyurl.com /3bed4w7h.

Gedeon, Kimberly. "Microsoft Edge Will Use AI to Add Real-Time Translation to Videos—What This Means for You." Mashable, May 21, 2024. https://tinyurl.com/2uwhj4jj.

Giattino, Charlie, Esteban Ortiz-Ospina, and Max Roser. "Working Hours." *Our World in Data,* n.d. https://tinyurl.com/4s7a6z8h.

Glaveski, Steve. "The Case for the 6-Hour Workday." *Harvard Business Review,* December 11, 2018. https://tinyurl.com/mvucx8ae.

González, David. "Laguna Beach HS Investigating Incident Involving AI-Generated Nude Photos of Students." *ABC7,* April 1, 2024. https:// tinyurl.com/34ykvm59.

Haidt, Jonathan. *The Anxious Generation.* New York: Penguin Press, 2024.

Harwood, Michelle. "AI Wrote the US Constitution, Says AI Content Detector." *Medium,* September 7, 2023. https://tinyurl.com/2f9b4d9c.

Heikkilä, Melissa. "How It Feels to Be Sexually Objectified by an AI." *MIT Technology Review,* December 13, 2022. https://tinyurl.com/5vfpu92e.

Heiser, Michael S. *The Unseen Realm: Recovering the Supernatural Worldview of the Bible.* Bellingham, WA: Lexham Press, 2015.

Hiebert, Paul. *Transforming Worldviews: An Anthropological Understanding of How People Change.* Grand Rapids, MI: Baker Academic, 2008.

Hiebert, Paul G., R. Daniel Shaw, and Tite Tiénou. *Understanding Folk Religion: A Christian Response to Popular Beliefs and Practices.* Grand Rapids, MI: Baker Books, 1999.

Himanen, Pekka. *The Hacker Ethic and the Spirit of the Information Age.* New York: Random House, 2001.

Hsu, Andrea. "Iceland Cut Its Workweek and Found Greater Happiness and No Loss in Productivity." *NPR,* July 6, 2021. https://tinyurl.com /2efsjpwr.

IBM Data and AI Team. "Shedding Light on AI Bias with Real World Examples." IBM.com. October 16, 2023. https://tinyurl.com/55nenfhc.

———. "Understanding the Different Types of Artificial Intelligence." IBM.com. October 12, 2023. https://tinyurl.com/2ved4vu4.

Imes, Carmen Joy. *Being God's Image: Why Creation Still Matters.* Downers Grove, IL: IVP Academic, 2023.

Johnson, Luke Timothy. *Prophetic Jesus, Prophetic Church: The Challenge of Luke–Acts to Contemporary Christians.* Grand Rapids, MI: Eerdmans, 2011.

Johnson Space Center Office of Communications. "NASA Humanoid Robot to Be Tested in Australia." NASA.gov, July 6, 2023. www.nasa.gov/centers-and-facilities/johnson/nasa-humanoid-robot-to-be-tested-in-australia/.

Khullar, Dhruv. "Talking to Ourselves." *The New Yorker*, March 6, 2023. 16-22.

Kissinger, Henry, Eric Schmidt, Daniel P. Huttenlocher, and Schuyler Schouten. *The Age of AI: And Our Human Future.* New York: Little, Brown, 2021.

Korpi, Todd. "The Digital Frontier of Mission." Digital Mission Consortia. Wheaton, IL: Wheaton College Billy Graham Center, June 2023.

———. "5 Ways We Get Evangelism Wrong and What We Can Do About It." *ChurchLeaders.Com* (blog), November 14, 2023. https://tinyurl.com/5bksrart.

———. "A Holy Priesthood: Cultivating Ecosystems for Missional Formation at Celebration Church." Doctor of Missiology Dissertation, Fuller Theological Seminary, School of Mission and Theology, 2022. www.proquest.com/openview/33cb3cdd68b8833915a182d4fbc10d9d/1.

———. "Renovating Pastoring." Substack newsletter. *Church Talk with Todd Korpi* (blog), September 21, 2023. https://toddkorpi.substack.com/p/renovating-pastoring.

———. *Your Daughters Shall Prophesy: Amplifying the Voice and Place of Christian Women.* Eugene, OR: Wipf & Stock, 2023.

Korynta, Emma. "'Art Will Never Be the Same:' Charlotte Artist Has Her Work Scraped by AI." WCNC Charlotte, December 20, 2023. https://tinyurl.com/yc74hha7.

Koyama, Kosuke. *Three Mile an Hour God.* London: SCM, 1979.

Larson, Jeff, Surya Mattu, Lauren Kirchner, and Julia Angwin. "How We Analyzed the COMPAS Recidivism Algorithm." *ProPublica*, May 23, 2016. https://tinyurl.com/3ztpjd28.

Latson, Jennifer. "When Daylight Saving Time Was Year-Round." *Time*, February 9, 2015. https://time.com/3695333/daylight-saving-time-wwii/.

Lines, Caleb J. *The Great Digital Commission: Embracing Social Media for Church Growth and Transformation.* Eugene, OR: Cascade Books, 2021.

Lytle, Julie Anne. *Faith Formation 4.0: Introducing an Ecology of Faith in a Digital Age.* New York: Morehouse, 2013.

MacArthur, John. "Social Injustice and the Gospel." *Grace to You* (blog), August 13, 2018. https://tinyurl.com/bdfbv29n.

Mauro, Gianluca, and Hilke Schellmann. "'There Is No Standard': Investigation Finds AI Algorithms Objectify Women's Bodies." *The Guardian*, February 8, 2023. https://tinyurl.com/4kpuyztb.

McDonald, Bruce, dir. *Creeped Out.* Season 2, episode 3, "Help." Aired May 8, 2019, on Netflix.

Moreau, A. Scott. *Contextualizing the Faith: A Holistic Approach.* Grand Rapids, MI: Baker Academic, 2018.

Munzinger, Andre. *Discerning the Spirits: Theological and Ethical Hermeneutics in Paul.* Society for New Testament Studies 140. Cambridge, UK: Cambridge University Press, 2010.

Newbigin, Lesslie. *The Gospel in a Pluralist Society.* Grand Rapids, MI: Eerdmans, 1989.

Nolan, Erin. "For Older People Who Are Lonely, Is the Solution a Robot Friend?" *The New York Times*, July 6, 2024. https://tinyurl.com/yckjp5sx.

Nouwen, Henri J. M. *Reaching Out: The Three Movements of the Spiritual Life.* Garden City, NY: Doubleday, 1975.

Okuda, Michael, and Denise Okuda. "From the Star Trek Archive: Communicators and PADDS." StarTrek.com, June 18, 2024. www.startrek.com/gallery/star-trek-archive-okudagrams.

Pfefferkorn, Riana. "Teens Are Spreading Deepfake Nudes of One Another. It's No Joke." *Scientific American*, June 10, 2024. https://tinyurl.com/mwu5syn4.

Quartz. "This App Is Trying to Replicate You." August 29, 2019. https://qz.com/1698337/replika-this-app-is-trying-to-replicate-you.

Rasenberger, Mary. "Opinion: As AI Is Embraced, What Happens to the Artists Whose Work Was Stolen to Build It?" *Los Angeles Times*, June 18, 2024. https://tinyurl.com/4msnfxkt.

replika.com. "Replika." Accessed July 18, 2023. https://replika.com.

Rollin, Bernard. "Animal Ethics and the Law." *Michigan Law Review First Impressions* 106, no. 1 (2008). https://tinyurl.com/56s35mw7.

Sanford, Alyxaundria. "Artificial Intelligence Is Putting Innocent People at Risk of Being Incarcerated." *Innocence Project*, February 14, 2014. https://tinyurl.com/3zhyjmdt.

Silver, David, Thomas Hubert, Julian Schrittwieser, Ioannis Antonoglou, Matthew Lai, Arthur Guez, Marc Lanctot, et al. "Mastering Chess and Shogi by Self-Play with a General Reinforcement Learning Algorithm." arXiv, Cornell University, December 5, 2017. https://tinyurl.com/2t8pp8f6.

Singer, Natasha. "Teen Girls Confront an Epidemic of Deepfake Nudes in Schools." *The New York Times*, April 8, 2024. https://tinyurl.com/32th84sc.

Spadaro, Antonio, and Maria Way. *Cybertheology: Thinking Christianity in the Era of the Internet*. New York: Fordham University Press, 2014.

Sundkler, Bengt. *The World of Mission*. Foundations of Mission Series. Grand Rapids, MI: Eerdmans, 1965.

Turnitin. "AI Writing," n.d. https://tinyurl.com/y9y7wkye.

U.S. Bureau of Labor Statistics. "Occupational Employment and Wage Statistics." May 2023. https://tinyurl.com/54vak9uf.

Van Engen, Charles. *God's Missionary People: Rethinking the Purpose of the Local Church*. Grand Rapids, MI: Baker, 1991.

Vella, Jane Kathryn. *Learning to Listen, Learning to Teach: The Power of Dialogue in Educating Adults*. Rev. ed. The Jossey-Bass Higher and Adult Education Series. San Francisco: Jossey-Bass, 2002.

Vincent, James. "Twitter Taught Microsoft's AI Chatbot to Be a Racist Asshole in Less than a Day." *The Verge*, March 24, 2016. https://tinyurl.com/4au4fwbz.

Walton, John H. *The Lost World of Adam and Eve: Genesis 2–3 and the Human Origins Debate*. Downers Grove, IL: IVP Academic, 2015.

———. *The Lost World of Genesis One: Ancient Cosmology and the Origins Debate*. Downers Grove, IL: IVP Academic, 2009.

Walton, John H., Victor H. Matthews, and Mark W. Chavalas. *The IVP Bible Background Commentary: Old Testament*. Downers Grove, IL: InterVarsity Press, 2000.

Ward, Marguerite. "A Brief History of the 8-Hour Workday, Which Changed How Americans Work." *CNBC*, May 3, 2017. https://tinyurl.com/6muna3t2.

Willard, Dallas. *Renovation of the Heart: Putting on the Character of Christ.* Colorado Springs, CO: NavPress, 2002.

Winter, Ralph D., Steven C. Hawthorne, Darrell R. Dorr, D. Bruce Graham, and Bruce A. Koch. *Perspectives on the World Christian Movement: A Reader.* Princeton, NJ: William Carey Publishing, 2009.

Wise, Justin. *The Social Church: A Theology of Digital Communication.* Chicago: Moody Publishers, 2014.

Witt, Emily. "The Future of Fertility." *The New Yorker*, April 17, 2023. www.newyorker.com/magazine/2023/04/24/the-future-of-fertility.

Woodward, J. R., and Dan White Jr. *The Church as Movement: Starting and Sustaining Missional-Incarnational Communities.* Downers Grove, IL: InterVarsity Press, 2016.

World Health Organization. "The True Death Toll of Covid-19: Estimating Global Excess Mortality," May 20, 2021. https://tinyurl.com/mrcem76c.

Wright. N. T. *Surprised by Hope.* San Francisco: HarperOne, 2008.

ABOUT THE AUTHOR

DR. TODD KORPI is a missiologist, pastor, and consultant driven by a passion to mobilize the church to thrive as a community of missionaries in today's world. With advanced degrees in missiology and global leadership, Todd has spent over two decades empowering churches to shape their mission-minded identities.

Todd and his wife, Tara, lead a ministry that provides resourcing, consultation, and training to empower churches and Christian organizations of all sizes to improve their effectiveness, align their mission, and empower people for the work of ministry.

Todd teaches missiology and leadership at Fuller Theological Seminary and Southeastern University, and he is founding Dean of Digital Ministries at Ascent College. He is director of the Digital Mission Consortia at the Wheaton College Billy Graham Center and works with OneHope. His work in digital ministry and innovative church planting has been featured in *Outreach Magazine* and Churchleaders.com, where he contributes as a thought leader on the church's role in a rapidly changing world. Todd's previous books include *Your Daughters Shall Prophesy* and *The Life-Giving Spirit*, both of which explore how faith communities can embrace their mission more fully.

Todd lives in the Chicagoland area with Tara and their three daughters. Together, they're dedicated to supporting a new generation of Christian leaders who are deeply rooted in their faith and equipped for the challenges of our time.

Connect with Todd on social media (@toddkorpi) or at www.toddkorpi.com.

Like this book?
Scan the code to discover more content like this!

Get on IVP's email list to receive special offers, exclusive book news, and thoughtful content from your favorite authors on topics you care about.

 InterVarsity Press